my
Dad's
got
Mojo

my Dad's got Mojo

He's the best dad ever!

GARY BERTWISTLE

Wrightbooks

First published 2010 by Wrightbooks
an imprint of John Wiley & Sons Australia, Ltd
42 McDougall Street, Milton Qld 4064

Office also in Melbourne

Typeset in Berkeley LT 12/15.4 pt

© Gary Bertwistle 2010

The moral rights of the author have been asserted

National Library of Australia Cataloguing-in-Publication entry:

Author:	Berwistle, Gary.
Title:	My dad's got mojo: he's the best dad ever! / Gary Bertwistle.
ISBN:	9781742469546 (pbk.)
Notes:	Includes index.
Subjects:	Father and child.
	Fatherhood—Psychological aspects.
	Fathers—Family relationships.
	Fathers—Handbooks, manuals, etc.
	Parenting—Handbooks, manuals, etc.
	Child rearing—Handbooks, manuals, etc.
Dewey Number:	306.8742

Cover design by Brad Maxwell

Front cover image © iStock Vectors
Back cover image © iStock Vectors
Diagram on p. 5 reproduced with the permission of Allen & Unwin

Printed in China by Printplus Limited

10 9 8 7 6 5 4 3 2 1

Disclaimer

The material in this publication is of the nature of general comment only, and does not represent professional advice. It is not intended to provide specific guidance for particular circumstances and it should not be relied on as the basis for any decision to take action or not take action on any matter which it covers. Readers should obtain professional advice where appropriate, before making any such decision. To the maximum extent permitted by law, the author and publisher disclaim all responsibility and liability to any person, arising directly or indirectly from any person taking or not taking action based upon the information in this publication.

Contents

Also by Gary Bertwistle

What Made You Think of That?
Thinking differently in business

Who Stole My Mojo?
How to get it back and live,
work and play better

The Keys to Creativity:
How to unlock your imagination and
creative potential

The Vibe:
The marketing handbook for every
product, service and industry

To the dads…
the good, the bad and the ugly

About the author

Gary Bertwistle is a dad. He's also one of Australia's leaders in thinking. He is a keynote speaker whose topics include the thinking behind creativity, innovation, marketing, brand and performance. In 2002 he opened Australia's first creative thinking venue at the Entertainment Quarter in Sydney, called the Ideas Vault, which is used by some of the country's biggest corporations for creative thinking, meetings, seminars and training sessions. He is the author of four books: *The Keys to Creativity*, *Who Stole My Mojo?*, *What Made You Think of That?* and *The Vibe*.

Gary is the co-founder of one of Australia's leading cycling foundations, the Tour de Cure, which raises money in an effort to cure cancer. The Tour de Cure has raised millions of dollars since its inception in 2007. Gary also founded the Day of Inspiration, an annual corporate fundraising event.

Winner of the TEC Speaker of the Year Award in 2007 and 2008, Gary is renowned for his simple and easygoing style, passion and drive in helping people to think differently about their life, family, business and mojo. Visit Gary at <www.garybertwistle.com>.

Introduction

I was a little hesitant about writing a book about being a great dad. I'm not a doctor, I don't have a PhD in child psychology and I haven't published research papers, run focus groups or worked with government agencies involved with children, schools or parents. However, the sheer number of dads (and mums) who approach me after my speeches on creativity, imagination and performance through mojo about raising children with mojo finally convinced me to put my thoughts down on paper.

When someone asks me what I do, I say I'm a dad. The next thing I tell people is that I absolutely love it! I started as a dad later in life (I was in my forties) and I'm pretty glad I did. If my little girl, Charley (who is now four years old), had arrived much earlier, I don't think I would have been able to really enjoy fatherhood and undertake the mental and physical gymnastics involved, and at the same time hold myself to the standards I value personally and in my business. I feel very fortunate to be a dad and I'm thankful for every day with my daughter. I'm a regular guy who is just trying to be the best dad I can be to raise a happy, healthy, creative child — someone with mojo and the ability to make her own decisions about her life.

I consider myself to be a keen observer of people and their behaviour, something that has been reinforced by my interests and my work; I constantly walk around with my eyes and ears open. In my life I have observed many happy, well-balanced, intelligent children — both prior to and after becoming a dad — and I have spent many hours watching and listening as kids engage with their parents. I've sat in cafes, restaurants, airports, kindergartens and on public transport, and I have seen some truly outstanding dads in action. I've also read some fascinating books about children and child behaviour, and about how you can bring up children to be their best.

My Dad's Got Mojo is a practical, easy-to-read guide to parental greatness for every dad — taking you from being a good dad to a great (or even an outstanding) one.

I hope that you enjoy it and that you will come back to it if and when you need to.

Some of what I say you may agree with. I also expect you may vehemently disagree with other things I say. All of which I'm okay with as long as it gets you thinking. If all you do as a result of reading this book is take the time to consider whether there's more you can do to create an environment for your child in which he can be the best he can be, then it's been a worthwhile investment of your time and money.

I live by the philosophy of Leonardo da Vinci, which is 'Simplicity is the ultimate sophistication', so I've tried to illustrate everything I say with real-life examples and stories to keep things relevant and simple.

Life is complicated and it would be unrealistic to expect that any of us should or will be able to do all the things in this book all of the time. Stuff happens, stuff that is often completely out of our control. As such, I've written this book with one goal in mind—to help you think differently about being a dad and create your own image of how you would like to be perceived in the eyes of your child or children. Remember, being the best dad ever centres on one person—you. It's about your behaviour and your attitudes, not your child's.

At the end of each chapter you'll find a checklist that you can go back to whenever you feel like you've lost your mojo or if you just need a reminder of what you can be doing to be a truly outstanding dad. In addition, as you go through the book you may want to jot down your own thoughts or notes — you'll find some blank pages at the back of the book that are there for this purpose.

Each of us has a unique set of circumstances and values, which is why I hope you will apply the tips, tools and ideas explored in this book to your own world, in your own time and in the way that you see fit. An executive running a multimillion-dollar company is different from a small business owner, who in turn is different from someone working for a delivery business, an office worker, a baker or a stay-at-home dad. Yet all have it in them to be the best dad ever in the eyes of their children.

Cupcakes in the cubbyhouse

One afternoon I was in our backyard cubbyhouse enjoying some freshly baked cupcakes with my then three-year-old daughter. She was serving me imaginary tea, and had been doing so for about forty-five minutes. The cupcakes were delicious, but the imaginary cups of tea were wearing a bit thin. I reached for my mobile phone with the intention of checking my email and at that moment I stopped myself and thought, 'What example am I setting? Is there anything more important than being here in the moment enjoying cupcakes with my daughter?'

I asked myself if I would ever look back and regret spending time with Charley instead of checking emails, sending text messages or making phone calls. The answer was a resounding NO! Right there in that moment, having cupcakes in the cubbyhouse was the most important thing in the world, not just for my little girl, but also for me.

The following day I presented to a group of corporate executives and by the time I finished it was mid afternoon. When one of the attendees asked me where I was headed next I told him I was going home to have cupcakes in the cubbyhouse. This man, who also happened to be a dad, thought that was fantastic and I was fortunate to be able to do it, and that he wished he could. Well, I thought at the time, if he truly wished it, he could make it happen.

We all create ceilings and barriers (either consciously or unconsciously) that prevent us from being a great dad. It is my hope that this book removes some of these barriers and allows more fathers to have the relationship with their kids that they desire and be the dad they want to be.

Their greatest inspiration

Every year I host a corporate event at the Four Seasons Hotel in Sydney for about 300 to 400 businesspeople. The Day of Inspiration is a full-day event where some of Australia's best keynote speakers and entertainers hit the stage to inspire a corporate audience with their secrets of achievement. In 2007, its first year, I invited the audience to write down and share who their greatest inspirations had been to date in their lives. Overwhelmingly this audience listed a parent. In fact, one of the attendees told me that the previous evening she had told her dad that he was the best dad ever. It is my hope that this book gets you thinking about how you can be the best dad ever in the eyes of your child.

My Dad's Got Mojo is about ensuring that you are setting the right tone and example for your children and creating the best environment you can, so that in years to come when someone asks your son or daughter who their greatest inspiration is you are at the top of their list.

Chapter 1

Being the best dad ever

If you bought this book or it has been kindly given to you, I'm thinking that you have an interest in knowing what it takes to be a truly outstanding dad. You're probably keen to find out some tips, tools and secrets to hearing the sentence that every dad wants to hear uttered by their little boy or girl: 'You're the best dad ever!' Well, join the club because I've been in that place and I'm still there today.

In this chapter I'm going to take you through some of the aspects of fatherhood that are key to being a truly great dad. It may be confronting. It may simply make you more aware of your role as a dad. If all it does is make you think about what sort of dad you want to be, I believe it's been a worthy investment of your time. With that in mind let's get started.

Standards and your identity

Most of us work with a group of people or a team. I bet you could name pretty readily a couple of people who do a good job and a couple of people who do a great job. I'm also sure that you would be able to identify the stars or the truly outstanding individuals in your company or team.

There is always that one person who stands out from the rest. Often it's not because of any additional knowledge or skills, it's more to do with attitude. It's the way they consistently approach the job and do those little things that are over and above what is expected of them. They turn up to meetings early and prepared. They stay back to ensure that the job is not just done, but that it is done to the best of their ability. They pore over a presentation to make sure it's right. They take the time to send a nice message to a staff member or client to show their appreciation or thanks. They're the people who do everything they can to make sure their job is in order before they go on holiday, so there are no nightmares while they are away.

People who hold themselves to a higher standard than those around them have their mojo going on. Good or great is simply not enough for these people, and they hold themselves to a higher standard than anyone else could expect from them. I believe a similar approach applies to being a dad.

Are you a good dad, a great dad or an outstanding dad? Being an outstanding dad is not necessarily about skill or knowledge. Indeed, it's nothing more complicated than knowing what sort of dad you want to be and under-taking the necessary steps to fulfil that vision.

Are you a good dad, a great dad or an outstanding dad?

Take, for example, a guy I met who was going through a tough time. His wife had recently left him and he said to me, 'I don't know why she left me. I was a good hus-band and a good dad'. This may seem harsh, but I asked him whether being a good dad or a good husband was enough? So often we do only what is required and believe that will be good enough.

To be a truly outstanding dad you need to have a vision of how you want things to pan out, and then be willing to put in the effort to achieve your goal. Don't be one of those dads who mistakenly believes that because he happens to be the major breadwinner, he is excused from doing those little extras. The long hours these dads spend at work and the time they put in at home on the laptop, the mobile or the BlackBerry 'for the good of the family' is not an acceptable excuse! Yes, being the breadwinner is an important role, but I believe that too often men's identity is inextricably entwined with their job. Rather than letting your job (and your success at that job) define you, I challenge you to begin building your primary identity around being a dad, a husband, a lover, a family man.

The outstanding dads I have met are the ones who put their family first, and then build their work commitments around that. Yes, we all need money in the bank to fulfil our basic needs and the goals of the family, but this should be a secondary priority. Your first priority should be to ensure that you live every moment in the present with your kids and partner. I know what you're thinking — you're run off your feet at work and you have to be there, your family needs the money to put food on the table each week, therefore your work commitments must take first place. I would suggest, however, that these two concepts are not mutually exclusive, and that they can in fact coexist quite comfortably — it is just a matter of perception.

I strongly believe that ceilings are what separate the good and the great dads from the outstanding dads, as you can see in the diagram opposite. I call this concept 'raising the roof'. By this I mean that to be an outstanding dad, you need to first remove the ceilings that are holding you back. The outstanding dads don't listen to that voice inside their head saying as they read this book, 'Yeah, yeah. Sure, Gary, it's okay for you'. Instead they say, 'What would need to change for me to become an outstanding dad and how soon can I get started?'

These ceilings are the excuses that we make for not holding ourselves to a higher standard. It's all the reasons we can't get to swimming training or take a single lunch time off to take our kids to the theatre or to playgroup. It's the reason you're at work until 8.30 pm on a regular basis or taking calls at 7 am at the breakfast table instead of engaging in a conversation about the day ahead with your children. It's how you justify spending so much time on the mobile phone while you're on holiday with your family. Sadly this story is all too familiar for many dads out there.

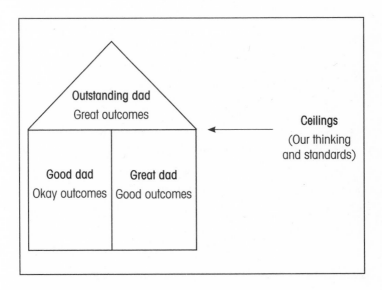

The good news is that these ceilings are nothing more than a belief system that translates into a lack of action and willpower to go the extra mile to become the best dad possible. The ceilings are just your thinking. To be an outstanding dad you need to change your thinking and then change your priorities. The first thing you should do is work out what a perfect world would look like for you and your kids in your home environment, and then work out what steps need to be taken to allow you to achieve that goal. Remember, it's all a choice. Spending time with your kids versus calls on your mobile—it really is as simple as that!

The dancer

Not only do we create our own ceilings, if we're not careful we can also instil this negative thought pattern in our kids. I was chatting to a group of people from Sydney's Creative Alliance of Learning and one of the members told a great story about his son, who is a dancer.

Think carefully about...the influence you can have on your kids' dreams and their future.

Although only a young boy, his son was reaching extraordinary heights with his dancing, and this dad wanted to encourage him. When it came time for his son's next big performance, he went along to rehearsals. While the boy was up on stage, his father was trying to act quite nonchalant, keeping an eye on his son but acting as if he was only half interested. After his son successfully performed a particularly tricky part of his routine, he left the stage very proud of himself, went over to his dad and said, 'Dad, did you see that?' His dad replied that he had. His son then said, 'What did you think? Pretty good, hey?' His dad said, 'Yes, it was good, but you're a bit of a show-off aren't you?' The boy looked at his father in surprise and said, 'Dad, dancing *is* showing off'.

This is a great example of how we can so easily plant negative voices inside our children's heads and create ceilings over them and what they can achieve. Whether we intend to or not, it can be a very dangerous thing to do. We can either ignite their creativity and individuality by fuelling their dreams or we can just as easily completely extinguish them—the choice is ours. Think carefully about the language you use and the influence you can have on your kids' dreams and their future.

How has fatherhood changed you?

During a drive to the southern highlands outside of Sydney I had the pleasure of talking to the creative director of one of Sydney's top radio stations about being a dad. We had been discussing children's learning and creative process, which are topics close to home for both of us, and after about an hour he turned and asked, 'What has changed you by being a dad?' I replied that there were two things that came to mind.

The first was curiosity. I love the fact that kids question the things we take for granted and that as a parent our own curiosity is sparked and encouraged in so many different ways by kids. Curiosity is one of the most important traits we can draw out of our children in their first five to seven years of life. It is curiosity that sets the stage for a child's creativity, problem solving and imagination, which can be used for any endeavour in life. Their persistent questioning and thirst for knowledge really does make us think. It makes us consider questions we had never before thought about and question things we take for granted.

The second thing that came to mind was how much your kids make you laugh. US talk-show host David Letterman summed it up best when he said, 'The thing they don't tell you about being a dad is how much [your kids] make you laugh'. If you're being serious more than you are laughing with your child, then you're missing the 'juice', the essence of having a wonderful relationship with your child. You're missing opportunities and, ultimately, setting an unbalanced tone in the home environment for your kids. They should make you smile, grin, giggle and sometimes even give you a good belly laugh.

My suggestion to you is that once in a while take the time to sit back, reflect and perhaps even record in a journal, diary or the blank pages at the back of this book details about the journey of your child or children as they're growing up. I would also recommend reflecting on the things that have changed you in a good way since becoming a parent. Writing these things down will reinforce what's great for you and what's made the biggest change to you, and chances are by reinforcing it you'll get more of it.

Do you keep your promises?

Raising children successfully is all about working within a consistent set of standards, beliefs and actions. By repeating something over and over, it builds patterns that over time form the beliefs and habits of your children.

It is, however, a two-way street. If you hope to instil certain beliefs and standards in your children, then they also have the right to expect the same from you. By using a consistent tone, consistent language and delivery with my daughter I feel I have been able to truly engage, rationalise and interact with her successfully. I also believe it has had a measurable impact on our relationship. If I say I'm going to do something within a certain time frame, then it has to happen. For example, if I say I'm going to pick Charley up from kindy at 5 pm, I'm always there before 5 pm to pick her up. If you make a promise and deliver on it, that consistency plays a big part in their mind.

Raising children successfully is all about working within a consistent set of standards, beliefs and actions.

Consistency gives kids stability, security and a level of expectation and trust with their parents. Don't think that because a child is only two or three years old she doesn't understand, because she does. We don't give children, especially our children, enough credit for what is going on inside their minds—they pick up on things much earlier than you think. If you'd like evidence of this, have a look at a terrific book called *What's Going on in There?*

by Lise Eliot. So if you make a promise or say you're going to do something, then do it. Give your kids the same respect you would to any other family member or friend when you give them your word.

Quite often people don't think about what it means to keep promises in a literal sense. For example, you explain to your kids why they must tell the truth to mum or dad, not to tell fibs. The next day you're at home playing with the kids, the home phone rings and your partner answers and calls out that it's Bill from down the road for you. If you then say, 'Tell him I'm not here', or 'Tell him I'm in the shower', this is a blatant lie and you're doing it in front of your children. Moments like this happen a lot of the time without conscious thought; however, you need to try to be more aware and catch yourself if you can because all of these things are going to be reflected back to you by your children. Why? Because you're their hero and they want to be like you, their dad!

It's about setting standards and keeping your promises on a consistent basis. So when you come home at night, remember to check yourself at the front door, disconnect from the day, engage and enjoy the privilege of truly sharing childhood with your kids.

The water bubbler

Unquestionably one of the most fulfilling and satisfying jobs I've done was sharing my experiences and what

I've learned with those who have the world at their feet. I had been asked to give a short talk about 'the hero within' to a leadership group in a primary school by one of the students there. My talk to the kids centred on the voice of doubt, disbelief, fear and hesitation that we often hear inside our heads. I asked them to say to themselves when they heard this voice: 'I can do it'. The kids loved this premise and we played for a while with that sentence.

The school's principal followed on from this with a brainstorming session with the children about who their heroes were and what attributes these heroes possessed. One little girl said that her hero was her grandmother and the attribute that made her a hero was that she gave her cookies every time she visited—out of the mouths of babes! Another young boy said that his hero was his brother who, despite being disabled, had managed to start his own IT company.

After we had identified the children's heroes and the attributes these heroes possessed, the principal broke the kids into groups to work on a roleplay as a way of presenting their findings to the rest of the school.

It was wonderful to watch this group of kids aged between five and ten brainstorming how they might go about roleplaying to illustrate their message. The children's parents had joined the session at this point, and I found their actions fascinating as they all jumped into the project with (and for) their kids. They started suggesting what the kids could do, what it would look like, what it would sound like and some even started putting together a script for them and began directing the performance.

I've learned that the best way for children to develop their imagination and curiosity is to let them create on their own. But parents being parents, we think that our job is to help children by putting our own ideas and thoughts into their minds. Kids have everything they need to create the next brilliant idea, and our job is to let that genius flourish. When you sit among children just practise stillness and silence; listen and observe what is going on around you. Appreciate exactly what creativity and innovation look like in the mind of a genius. I commented to one of the fathers watching that he should get the name and address of one of the kids in the group because in ten years' time that young person had the potential to be running his own business!

Kids have everything they need to create the next brilliant idea, and our job is to let that genius flourish.

Some of the ideas these kids came up with were brilliant. In fact, the vice-principal told me that several months earlier one of the children had suggested putting ice-cream buckets under the water bubblers to recycle water. The children were then asked to bring ice-cream buckets to school, which they placed under the water bubblers so that when somebody drank from the bubbler the excess water would fall into the buckets. This water was then used on the herb gardens, flowers and plants the children were growing around the school. In the lead-up to Mother's Day the herbs were harvested, wrapped in pretty paper and given to the children's mothers. As you can imagine the mothers were delighted to receive these presents grown by their children. I thought the story was fabulous and really showed the initiative that these little kids possess.

The challenge, as Picasso said, is to carry that genius into adulthood. We as adults need to learn when to speak and when to be quiet to allow our children to blossom into tomorrow's problem solvers. Next time you want to jump in and solve a problem for your children, think of the water bubblers. Your children are brighter, more creative and more innovative than you give them credit for.

Run, Daddy, run!

One sunny spring afternoon my daughter and I had been running from one side of the backyard to the other for about twenty minutes. First we chased each other, then we ran next to each other, and then we crossed over the middle slapping hands. By this time I was beginning to get a bit out of breath. Charley, however, was having the time of her life and every time she reached the end of the yard she'd hoot with laughter and call out, 'Let's go again! Run, Daddy, run!'

My mind started moving on to what else I still had to do that day, what time it was and who I had to call.

Then I heard the voice of motivational speaker Terry Hawkins echoing in my mind. No, I wasn't experiencing paranormal activity; I was just recalling the words I had heard the previous day at the Day of Inspiration, the corporate event I run at the Four Seasons Hotel in Sydney each year. Terry is renowned for her energy, passion and succinct messages that get people to move.

During her keynote speech Terry let the audience in on a secret that had had a profound influence on her life. As the audience waited in complete silence, Terry said, 'Ask people what they want and give it to them'. Sounds simple doesn't it? Ask people what they want and give it to them. Ask a customer what they want in customer service and give it to them. Ask your employees what they want (within reason) and give it to them. Ask your partner what they want and give it to them. Quite often the things people want are the simplest things and these are the things that tend to get pushed aside or completely overlooked.

In the backyard with Charley I heard Terry's voice ringing in my ears saying, 'Ask Charley what she wants and give it to her'. It was quite clear what Charley wanted—she wanted me to run, daddy, run. With that in mind, I continued to run. Soon after (to my considerable relief) Charley also began to tire and it was time to sit down and talk to the dogs. It really did make me think about how quickly I was ready to bail on an activity that held Charley completely enthralled.

In the brilliant book *Einstein Never Used Flash Cards*, authors Kathy Hirsh-Pasek and Roberta Michnick Golinkoff claim that the two most important things we can give a child between the ages of nought and seven are curiosity and play. I've read this book a number of times and keep going back to it to remind myself to feed and foster the imagination and creativity of children through curiosity. As parents we tend to think that we need to be doing things to be

...the two most important things we can give a child...are curiosity and play.

achieving something — that is, we often confuse activity with accomplishment. Many of us believe that if we are not being productive and getting ourselves organised, moving forward or achieving our goals, then it's not time well spent. I challenge you to consider this: in a child's world, the most valuable time you can spend is in play.

What Charley wanted me to do was to keep playing. I, on the other hand, was working out what needed to be done, to tick things off my list and make myself feel like I was making good use of the afternoon. However, it was actually my running backwards and forwards all those times across the backyard that was achieving the most important thing in the world at that point in time for my daughter.

Hirsh-Pasek and Michnick Golinkoff wrote the book in part to counterbalance the current popular thinking of parents that if children are just playing, they're not moving forwards, they're not progressing as human beings. This particular theory has been proven to be incorrect. Children learn best through curiosity and by playing. Ask them what they want and give it to them. Kids want to play, nothing more, nothing less—they want to be kids.

Modern-day parenting being what it is, however, we tend to buy ever-increasing numbers of 'educational toys' and flash cards, and take our young children to classes of every sort in an attempt to make them better human beings with a better education and higher intelligence. You don't need all these tools and artificial stimulation to give your child a head start in life. Keep things simple and allow them the space to use their own sense of curiosity, imagination and playfulness to enjoy their childhood. School will come soon enough!

Monkey see, monkey do

Over the years I've presented at thousands of team-building gatherings, conferences and board meetings all over the country and overseas. In doing so I've noticed that prior to the structured sessions, people tend to mill around outside discussing their business and personal lives. One thing that has struck me over and over is that these people often talk for ten minutes or so about their business life with facts, figures, stories and problems. However, when attention is turned to their lives away from the office, more often than not they say, 'Yeah, things are okay. It's just more of the same'. I find this quite sad. Now, perhaps they say this because they are surrounded by workmates, but I would hope they have more to share than just a line or two, even in this environment.

There is a danger in building your whole identity around work, as though it is the most important and significant thing in your world. Not only does it give undue weight to your work life in the big scheme of things, this situation can often leave an individual adrift if they suddenly lose their job.

The other thing I find is alarming is the message it sends to your children. If you can sit there and talk for ten or twenty minutes about your work life, but your personal life is just 'much of the same', then you can't be providing a very stimulating, exciting, enlightening or varied environment for your kids. Children need variety and stimulation to develop their curiosity. Go back through your diary for the last month—if you were asked what was significant to you in that period, would it be much of the same? Your kids want to be like you, so if they see you doing the same thing every day—getting up at 7 am, rushing breakfast, dashing to the office, getting home at 7 pm and walking in the door on the mobile phone—then they will still want to be like you, as sad as that might be.

There is a danger in building your whole identity around work, as though it is the most important and significant thing in your world.

On the other hand, if your children see you training and competing in a half marathon for the first time or taking up a new hobby, then that sends a different kind of message. If your children see you offering to work at the school fete, or helping with the fundraising or building of an extension to the church, then that sends a message too. If they see you taking cooking courses or learning to play an instrument, then that also sends a message to them. If they see you going to the gym a couple of days a week, and then on the weekend going kayaking, cycling or on a bushwalk, this is another message.

In the same way, if your children are always seeing you reading books, whether they are fiction or nonfiction, then they are going to want to reflect those same habits. For them, you are a mirror. If your world is full of much of the same week after week, month after month, year after year, then take this as a wake-up call and an opportunity to change this situation.

Find the hedgehog and find your imagination

I was on a flight from Australia to London in 2009 when I watched a movie called *Imagine That* starring Eddie Murphy. I thoroughly enjoyed the movie and thought it had some terrific lessons for dads. The story is about a stockbroker, played by Murphy, who is caught up in the typical corporate day-to-day whirlwind of goals, budgets, clients, competition and achievement. He was successful in every way at work, but it was another story at home. His marriage had failed and he didn't have a relationship with his daughter.

Over the course of the movie Murphy is forced to take more responsibility for his child and consequently spends more time with her. The little girl introduces her dad to the characters living in her imaginary world. With his career heading in a downward spiral, he finds the solution to his problems in the world dreamt up by his daughter. Naturally, he is sucked in by the results achieved with the help of the imaginary friends and he heads off on a journey of success and greed. It's not until the end of the movie that Murphy realises what his daughter's imagination has really given him — the chance to have a relationship with her.

During a speech to a large infrastructure corporation in Berkshire in the UK, I had been talking about creativity and mojo in children and the responsibilities we have as parents to raise princes and princesses of possibility. A dad in the audience raised his hand and told the story of the hedgehog. He said one day he was walking in a forest with his three-year-old daughter when she stopped, turned around and said, 'Dad, look at this, it's a hedgehog!' Her dad looked everywhere for the hedgehog but there was none. He then realised his daughter was holding a pine cone in her hand and saying, 'Look, right here, it's a hedgehog'. At that point the dad realised that his little girl had a wonderfully vivid imagination and his job from that point forward was to always find the hedgehog. I told him to hire *Imagine That* as it would be a perfect context to assist him.

As dads, if we can find the hedgehog with our own children, not only will it build a closer and more enjoyable relationship with our kids, but it will also help in every aspect of our work life. No matter what you do during your day, whether it's working in a corporation, running your own business, helping out at a not-for-profit organisation or coordinating a social mahjong group, if you can see the hedgehog you will benefit immeasurably. The problem is most dads don't take the time, make the effort or truly believe in the hedgehog.

The biggest challenge for us as dads is to let go. To truly see the hedgehog you have to let go of being the adult, let go of being right and get into the world that we used to know, back when we were kids. We need to be completely in the moment, to muck around, play, laugh and use our imagination. The hardest part is letting go of what others will think when we are childlike and having fun. Letting go of how we're supposed to act, and how we think others expect us to act, is also one of the biggest barriers in front of us as adults in brainstorming sessions or problem-solving meetings for our customers and clients. We can learn a lot from our kids. Make it your mission to find the hedgehog.

Compartmentalise

Recently I had coffee with a good mate of mine who is a truly outstanding dad. Not only does he run a successful advertising organisation, he's also a father of five, raises huge amounts of money for charity, is on a number of committees and still has a well-balanced life. So when writing this book I turned to the guy who I thought was doing better than most and I asked him for his top tips for being an outstanding dad. The first thing he said was, 'You won't always be perfect. You have to accept that there are times when things will get out of control and you'll have to deal with them as best you can'. Accepting this truth is essential for all parents.

One way of dealing with all these commitments is to compartmentalise. My mate explained how he does this. 'I work really hard to ensure that when I'm at work I'm productive and I get as much done as possible. I com-partmentalise—I set aside time for emails, time for creative thinking, time for meetings with the team, and time out for myself to read and explore unrelated content to fire up my imagination.' When he's doing those things he avoids distractions.

He said the same compartmentalisation works with his children and his partner. He creates time for his kids and when he's with them, he's really with them. One of the greatest challenges he found was disconnecting from his BlackBerry while he's with the children. However, in doing so, it has made an enormous difference to his relationship with his kids and the enjoyment he gets from his interaction with them. If he knows he's got a weekend of commitments at football games and birthday parties, then he cleans his slate as much as possible by the end of the week, so he's not forced to multi-task while with the kids. He can just be with them and not think about anything else.

In order to compartmentalise you have to spend time planning and getting organised. If you know you have a busy week, then work out what needs to be done and by when to free yourself up. If you can manage to compartmentalise, it is a wonderful way of being 'present' whatever you happen to be doing.

I personally find this technique valuable when I'm writing. I might think about a chapter or an article I need to write for a number of days, or even a week, but then I set aside some time when I'm able to immerse myself in it for an hour or two and for whatever reason my brain seems to be ready to go at that time. But if you don't plan for it, prepare for it and work to free up that time, something always gets in the way. Whether it's half an hour at the park or an afternoon watching football, the important thing is that during that time you won't be doing other things—business will be taken care of before or after you are there.

...if you don't plan for it, prepare for it and work to free up that time, something always gets in the way.

The same should be applied to making time for your partner. It's important for us to compartmentalise to be one-on-one with our partner, away from children, work, technology and distractions. Time when it's just hours with our partner to sit, reconnect, talk and share.

The mojo master

The day the world lost Australia's Crocodile Hunter, Steve Irwin, in 2006 was a sad day. I don't think too many people would disagree with me when I say that Steve Irwin had mojo! When Steve visited our lounge rooms via the television or was interviewed on radio, he brought mojo to our world. He had enough zest, passion, humour, love and commitment to fill an entire household. In an interview not long after his death, Terri, Steve's wife, commented that he really was an eternal child.

Although he had to get up every day at 4 am to tend to the animals at Australia Zoo, he would always go back to the house to have breakfast with the kids while Terri got organised and tidied up. No sooner had she finished than Steve would be playing with the kids, messing up the recently made beds and making cubby houses with the blankets, leaving the kids' bedrooms once again in chaos. But that was just the way he was. He lived for the moment and loved to have fun, throwing aside the generally accepted rules of behaviour for a grown man.

Often the most successful people are driven and goal-oriented (myself included). I'll never forget seeing that interview with Terri and thinking about how my own world was very rule-driven in a lot of respects, and that I must try to be more like Steve Irwin and have more fun with life. Since then I have been more childlike, I take life less seriously and I make having fun an important part of what Charley and I do together—laughing, playing, wrestling, giggling and doing the silly things that kids do during their childhood. And boy have there been some rewards. I've never laughed so much, felt so good or been so in love as with my daughter.

There are so many lessons we can take from Steve Irwin, but the one I will take away is this one. When you get the chance, grab your little boy or girl, mess up the bed and build a cubbyhouse—really have some fun. Not only will you have a ball, but your kids will love it!

Mojo checklist

▢ Have you made your first priority in your diary your family?

▢ Have you changed your thinking and are you holding yourself to a higher standard as a dad?

▢ Are you leading by example for your kids?

▢ Are you keeping your promises?

▢ Are you providing a varied and stimulating environment for your kids?

▢ Have you changed the language you use with your kids—that is, are you being encouraging and supportive?

▢ Are you letting your kids do things for themselves, rather than stepping in and doing things for them?

□ Are you fostering your child's imagination and curiosity?

□ Are you letting go and using your imagination?

□ Are you taking life less seriously?

□ Are you playing with your kids more often and bringing out your own child within?

Chapter 2

Putting first things first

In today's fast-paced, hi-tech world it's easy to get caught up in the ceaseless business cycle. The 'CrackBerry', wi-fi and the global economy mean work doesn't stop on Friday and start again on Monday — we're constantly connected to and engaged with our job. But you're doing it all for your family, and that's what matters, right? Wrong. In the whirlwind of meetings, emails, phone calls and deadlines too many dads have forgotten what's really important in life.

It's time to take a long, hard look at your priorities. It's time to disconnect from work and reconnect with your wife or partner and your kids. This chapter will give you the tools you need to get back on track and put your family first. Don't miss out on your kids' childhood—you'll never get it back.

The main thing

During a speech I was giving to a group of CEOs it dawned on me how many parents think they are 'with' their children when they spend time with them, but they're not really there at all. One CEO had related a story about how he had been on holiday with his family the week prior. On arrival at the island resort he had received an email on his BlackBerry from his head office in the United States alerting him that, due to the economic crisis and the fall of the Aussie dollar, his company's profit had fallen from $6 million to less than $2 million in a matter of days. He said, 'You can imagine I spent the next four days trying to find extra savings for the bottom line and consequently was always on my phone, emailing and calling to try to rectify the problem. It wasn't much of a holiday, but the kids had a good time, and that's the main thing'. Actually, I don't agree. It's *not* the main thing.

Each Wednesday I take Charley to swimming lessons. The area where I sit overlooks the pool so I can see Charley and her classmates and watch the fun unfold as she learns to swim. I always ensure that Charley can see me at any given time. I can't count the number of times when she has looked up during the lesson, waved to me with a huge smile on her face as if to say, 'Hey, Dad, did you see that?' Thankfully, yes, I did see it — I haven't missed a minute. Unfortunately, I can't say the same for many of the other mums and dads. They seem to take the swimming lesson as an opportunity to put their head in a magazine or newspaper, check their emails or chat on the phone.

Some time ago I gave a speech on creativity to a group of lawyers in Adelaide. I talked about the importance of creativity and the responsibility we have as parents to raise our children to be princes and princesses of possibility. One of the lawyers, who was also a dad, came up to me during the morning tea break and said, 'You've made me realise that often when I think I'm at home with my little boy, I'm not really home at all. Although we're in the same house together, I'm always too busy on my laptop or my mobile phone to engage with my little fella. Just the other day he told me how much he enjoys roleplaying and activities, yet looking back I realise how little time I do that with him. I'm always distracted. When I'm at home I need to be at home with him, engaging in whatever activity he wants to do'.

Don't miss out on your kids' childhood — you'll never get it back.

Granted, there are times for playing and times when you need to take care of business. Just don't kid yourself and think that because you're in the same building, you're doing the right thing and being with your child. If you've taken your child to the park but spent the whole time on your mobile, don't kid yourself and think that you're actually with your child. When your child sees you on your mobile phone, he knows.

Recently I was talking to a mum about my experiences at the pool and she related the same story. She said that she had taken her little boy to the pool for a lesson. He had done something that he thought was pretty cool and when he got out of the pool he said, 'Mum, you should have seen it—I went underwater! But you didn't see it because you were on your mobile phone'. She said she felt crushed and disappointed in herself for allowing this to happen and she vowed that it would not happen again.

When I was a kid I used to play cricket. During the matches if I did anything that I thought was significant with the bat, the ball or in the field, the first thing I did was look over to my dad to check that he'd seen it. When you're a kid, the people you most want to impress are your parents. Wanting recognition, praise and encouragement may seem simple, but quite often the things that mean the most to kids are the simple things. Kids don't overcomplicate things, they keep it simple—all they want is mum and dad there, watching and supporting them.

Next time you go to the park or the pool, look around and see how many parents aren't really there. In the first five to seven years of your child's life, the most important thing you can do is be with him, in the moment. Just because you've taken the kids on holiday, it doesn't mean you're with them and it doesn't mean they're having a good time. The main thing is engaging with your children, playing with them face to face and being in the moment. Just because they're two-and-a-half or three years old doesn't mean they don't know when you're really there and when you're not. Kids always know.

Stop and smell the sunflowers

Phil is a friend of mine who rides with the Tour de Cure, the cycling foundation I co-founded. Phil and I spend a lot of time on the road together, and I had the privilege of riding and climbing some of the mountain peaks with him during a trip to Europe to see the Tour de France. Phil only stayed with us for a couple of days before departing with his family on a well-earned break. He is the CEO of a successful global organisation and one of those people you look at and just know that they have their life in order.

He sent me an interesting email on his return from France. He said he had gone for a ride with his son, Max. While cycling Max and Phil came across an incredible field of sunflowers. It was yellow for as far as the eye could see. Phil decided to stop for a moment and suggested to Max that he step into the sunflowers so he could take a photo. Hesitant at first, Max finally put down the bike and headed into the field.

When they started riding again, Max turned to Phil and said, 'Dad, this is awesome! This is the longest bike ride we've ever done. We never do this at home—you're always too busy'. The last line of Phil's email was: 'How's that for a wake-up call?' Phil is someone who has it together, but sometimes we all miss the little things. We're so busy trying to do all the right things for all the right people for all the right reasons that we miss out on some of the more important stuff, such as setting an example and spending time engaging with our kids.

I'm pleased to say that Phil took the wake-up call to heart and has made some significant changes to address the situation with his kids. Phil was wise enough to do so, but many people aren't. Remember the sunflowers in your lives, too!

Slow down!

On one occasion when I took Charley for her swimming lesson I noticed a businessman dressed in a full suit, striding purposefully away from the pool while talking on a mobile phone. At the time it seemed odd that someone in a suit with no swimming or gym kit would be walking away from the pool, but I put it to the back of my mind. He returned to the pool deck a short time later to collect his son, who was having a swimming lesson too. He reached down into the pool and grabbed his son out of the water before rushing him off to get dressed and out to the car.

I sat there looking at this little boy and feeling a great deal of sorrow for him. His father obviously had so many important things going on at work that he couldn't afford to take the time to talk to his son, let alone share the experience of what had happened during his lesson. There were so many things not right about this picture, the least of which was the effect that these sorts of episodes, if repeated on a consistent basis, can have on the creativity, spirit and mojo of his child.

In research presented in the ABC television show *Life at 1*, parents were asked how often their household was stressed. In most cases the response was 'always' or 'often'. Every household is rushed or pressured for time at some point, but when it becomes a constant stress it can damage a child's brain.

We're so busy trying to do all the right things for all the right people...that we miss out on some of the more important stuff...

When a child is stressed the body produces adrenalin, and if the child remains stressed, the body starts to produce a chemical called cortisol. Cortisol is released by excessive stress and shuts down the areas of the brain that control memory, thinking and immunity. This constant stress and level of cortisol slows the development and growth of the brain. When a child is one year old, she will have developed fifty trillion connections in her brain. By the time the child is three years old these connections have increased to almost 1000 trillion. However, it is around this time that the brain begins to lose the connections that it is not using.

When a child is constantly stressed the brain shuts down those parts that are not essential to cope with the high stress level. The areas that are shut down are those largely responsible for thinking and for the development of creativity, imagination, problem-solving skills and ideas. As a result, the lower part of the brain develops strong emotional connections and, in some cases, the child is more likely to become aggressive, hateful, lacking in remorse and unable to understand the consequences of his actions.

Healthy brain development is not about using flash cards and listening to Mozart, it's about providing a consistently warm and loving environment. Do this and you will set your child on the path to happiness. Bringing the right spirit into the life of your child is as simple as the act of cuddling and cradling your child and, most importantly, establishing eye contact with them. A child that is loved and nurtured develops strong attachments and is more likely to be a healthy, happy, outgoing, contributing member of both your family and society, and have a zest for life.

There are two other quite startling footnotes worth mentioning. In *Life at 1*, it was noted that those professionals who worked long hours scored themselves poorly when asked to rate themselves as a parent. There are two issues here: first, the standards you hold yourself to as a mum or a dad and, second, your priorities. The second note from the documentary is that there is a link between childhood obesity and the amount of exercise done by the child's parents. Before you put down this book, think about how much exercise you've done in the last fortnight and whether or not you are leading by example. Because if your mojo isn't working, you can be sure your child's isn't either.

Look up

I've learned countless lessons since becoming a dad and spending time with my daughter. One of the most unexpected lessons was taking the time to stop and look around. Whenever we walk to kindy, Charley will say, 'Hey, Daddy, look at that!' and point up to the sky at the jet stream behind a plane, a bat hanging from a tree, a balloon slowly sailing across the sky or a pretty pink flower. Where most parents are concerned primarily with getting from point A to point B as quickly and efficiently as possible to cram more in to their day, children take the time to look around and, more importantly, to look up. So often Charley will see something on the trunk of a tree, in the sky or on our ceiling at home. Children teach us to look around and observe, and this is one of the most powerful traits that any of us can foster. It helps us unlock our great ideas and fuels our creativity, innovation and imagination in all aspects of our life.

When you take the time to tilt your eyes skyward two things happen. Firstly, you tend to relax, drop your shoulders and breathe. Secondly, 45 per cent to 55 per cent of us learn and process information visually. By taking the time to look up, you're relaxing and accessing the visual part of your mind, which is a stepping stone to accessing your imagination and creativity. Kids do it automatically, but as they get older we teach them to become more task-oriented and suck the creative genius out of them. We prevent them from looking up as we tear from job to job and task to task in order to be more productive and seemingly more successful.

Something else that happens when you take the time to look up is that you also take time to disconnect and ponder. When kids look up they're not looking for anything in particular, they just look up to see what's there. Children are born geniuses and this is one of the tools they use to foster that genius.

Next time you're walking with your kids to kindy, to the park, to the shops or to school, halve the pace that you're walking. In fact, let them set the pace, and if they want to dawdle let them dawdle. Spend some time, like your children, looking up and about to see what's there. Quite often when you see people going to and from meetings or on their lunch break, or going to and from work, they are so intent on getting to where they need to go they forget there's a whole world of activity going on above them. Residential, commercial, industrial and leisure activities all happen above our eye line that we just don't see or ponder. Take a lesson from your children and look up.

Unconditional love

In 2008 former cricketer, activist and Pakistani politician Imran Khan was in Australia as a special guest at an awards night. He was interviewed by Andrew Denton on the program *Enough Rope* and asked about his mother and the relationship he had with her. Khan said she gave him unconditional love that gave him a great deal of security in life. He knew that whatever he did, his mother would always love him.

This is a great premise for any parent to consider. When we think of unconditional love we often think of it going from children to parents. Babies and young children give parents absolute unconditional love. When it goes the other way it's the parents who accept children's ideas, imagination and creativity for exactly what it is. It's all that we do to them through language, barriers, beliefs and conditional love that takes the genius out of children.

Spend some time, like your children, looking up and about to see what's there.

Unconditional love is admiring a child's art, no matter what it is or what they've drawn, and appreciating it for what it is. It's asking children about their dreams, aspirations and hopes with true interest and true engagement. It's being in the moment with children as you discuss their imagination and creativity, and rewarding their curiosity, persistence and courage when they try new things, new thinking and new ideas. Unconditional love is accepting how children see the world and not always forcing our view of what society thinks is right onto them.

It's evident that this unconditional love set up a wonderful belief system for Imran Khan, who is arguably one of the best test cricketers Pakistan has ever had, and he has set his vision on helping to change his country for the better.

Another example of the product of unconditional love is the incredible story of actor John Travolta. In an interview he told how he and his mum would read scripts together at night in bed, and how his parents would sit for hours with a glass of wine and a cigar and watch him perform. That is what gave him the confidence in his early performances. He said they constantly told him that he was wonderful. On one occasion he went to an audition and was told to get out of the business. Travolta just thought the interviewers were crazy. In his mind nothing could ruin his career in acting—and this was before he made the big time. There's a difference between making false promises and giving children the belief and encouragement to be the best they can be. Our job as parents is to fan the spark, which becomes a little fire, which when encouraged becomes a blazing fire.

Are you focused on the right things?

In 2008 I presented to the training arm of the British Navy at the farmhouse of champion British athlete Sally Gunnell. Sally is an Olympic and Commonwealth Games medallist, world record holder, and European and World Champion. While at her farmhouse I noticed a number of her gold medals and photos of her success on the wall. This reminded me of a book I had read, *Mind Games* by Jeff Grout and Sarah Perrin, which made reference to Sally. It said she asked herself two questions each time she went to the blocks to compete in the women's 400 metre race. She would ask, 'Am I focused?' and 'Am I focused on the right things?'

I have taken a lot from these quotes since reading them and meeting Sally. I quite often stop myself before a speech or a cycling session and ask myself those two questions. I also use them as a handy tool when going home in the evening, before getting out of my car to go inside to my family. Often at the end of a busy day of travelling or a hectic day in the office, we tend to take work home with us. As we walk in the front door we're still in work mode, and as a result, our children, partner and household chores are a distraction and in most cases an annoyance.

I've spoken to a few dads who have learnt to break up the journey from the office to the front door by doing an activity to help snap them out of their work day. One dad has to drive past Sydney Harbour to get home. He often pulls off the road, parks by the harbour and puts on some relaxation music, just for five minutes, to break the journey. During that time he farewells the business day and looks forward to getting home. Another dad pulls into the driveway, turns on some music and sits in the car for a few minutes to allow himself to switch modes. Another goes straight from the front door, after saying hello to his wife and kids, to his bedroom, has a shower and puts on his trackpants. At that point he's washed off the day and is ready to be with his family.

Don't be one of those parents whose focus is on everything but their child. I once took Charley to the park and there was another dad there with his daughter. Sadly, this dad was not at all interested in what his little girl was doing. He was making calls and checking messages on his phone. What was interesting was that this little girl kept running around Charley and me, and pretending to fall over. She would then exclaim very loudly, 'Oh, I just fell over!' It was obvious that she was craving attention. She was a beautiful little girl with a lovely nature, but she was lacking the attention she wanted from her father. Perhaps her dad would notice her if she emailed him a photo of herself and he could see it on his mobile phone.

By not being in the moment with our kids we're...missing out on the juice of engaging and playing with them...

The even sadder part of this story is that this guy probably went to the pub that night or to work the next week and told everyone how he took his daughter to the park on the weekend. Sure, you took your little girl to the park, but you weren't in the park with her; she wasn't your focus. A lot of you reading this may be shaking your head and thinking, 'I can't believe he did that', but take a good look at yourselves because far too many of us are doing the same thing. This is an intrinsic issue for us dads. By not being in the moment with our kids we're not only depriving them of the attention they deserve, we're also missing out on the juice of engaging and playing with them in their most formative years.

So many people say that kids grow up before you know it, and it's little wonder if you're not paying attention to what's going on. We're all guilty of it, and it may not be something you're able to achieve every day, but make it a priority. Listen to what they're saying, watch what they're doing, smile at them and see yourself reflected in their face. I can guarantee you will also have a huge amount of fun, getting back to the innocence, mystery and curiosity of being a child.

Work out what you can put into your trip home that takes you from businessman to family man. I would suggest asking yourself 'Am I focused?' and 'Am I focused on the right thing?' If you're still focused on work, business issues, office dramas or your to do list, your children will pick up on it and most certainly your partner will know that you're not actually home yet. It's not how much time you spend with them, but how much time you spend truly engaged and present. These questions are a handy way to ensure that at any given time you're focused and, more importantly, you're focused on the right things.

How you focus on the right things is entirely up to you. Whether it's putting on a piece of music before getting out of your car, closing the door to your office and thinking about the evening ahead, reading a book on the bus or train, or pausing for sixty seconds before you put the key in the door, it's important for you to stop, reflect on the day, ensure you have created an action plan for the next morning so that you don't need to worry about it. Your mobile phone or BlackBerry should be switched off and you should be thinking about the most important people in your life—your children and your partner. Believe me, your family will notice the change and you will be rewarded tenfold through this investment of one, five or ten minutes of refocusing.

Have you lost your mojo?

Whenever you feel like you're losing your mojo as a dad, come back to the following list. It's a reminder of the things you need to be doing to be the best dad ever in the eyes of your child:

- *Visualise*. Picture what your perfect world or perfect relationship would look like with your children. How much time would you spend with them? What would you be doing? What would you hear them say? How would they feel being with you?

- *Make your kids a priority*. In this day and age, for most dads if it's not in your diary, it's not going to happen. Make sure that the first thing that goes into your diary for the week ahead is the time you'll be spending with your kids and what you'll be doing with them. Your family should be your highest priority. After all, if everything in your world went pear-shaped, I'm sure you'd agree the most important thing for you to take care of would be your family. Don't they deserve to have time with you? Remember, it's not how much time you spend with them, but that you are in the moment with them, enjoying it. Kids just want to see that their dad is engaged in the moment.

▫ *Compartmentalise*. Go through your diary and block out time for your kids, your partner, exercise, meetings and so on. Once it's compartmentalised, you have to ensure that you can have the time completely free, not only physically but mentally, to be in the moment. This is the essential tool for all time management and priority planning. Also allow time to create and be inspired. To plan ahead and compartmentalise you may need to say no to some things that aren't a priority. When Stephen Covey talked about time management in his best-selling book *The Seven Habits of Highly Effective People*, he said to make the best decisions and choices about your time, you may need to say no to some things—just do it nicely.

▫ *Relax*. When you're with your family they need to know that you're relaxed and not worrying about other things you think you should be doing. It's comforting to know that you have prioritised your time and blocked out that moment during an afternoon, early morning or evening to play, create, watch or involve your children in activity. If you're not relaxed about doing what you're doing, it means you haven't planned properly, you haven't compartmentalised and you certainly haven't prioritised your time. You can't do two things at once (although the female brain seems to be able to cope better with this than the male brain!). You're either in the moment or you're not. You're either relaxed or you're not. When you start to get distracted and worried, and feel like you should be doing something else, just consider this question: in this moment, what is the best use of your time when you consider your priorities in life?

This is not a list of things you have to do; rather, it's more of a checklist to come back to when you do feel as though things are running off the rails. It's not always going to be smooth sailing. Things will happen that are out of your control. The road ahead is going to get bumpy and sometimes take a turn for the worst. Just remember that there are things you can do to get back on track and bring the mojo back into your family life. Stuff's going to happen—accept it. However, if it happens all the time and it has been for a number of years, you need to take action. Just know that at any given time you can make choices about how you allocate your time.

Mojo checklist

▫ When you're with your children, are you really there, in the moment, with them?

▫ Are you providing a warm and loving home environment that's free from stress?

▫ Do you take the time to stop and look around—to look up—when you're outside, spending time with your child?

▫ Is the love you give your child unconditional?

▫ Are you focused and are you focused on the right things?

Chapter 3

Understanding how your little one learns

Something most parents don't realise is that children learn in different ways. Learning styles are something I explore when discussing creativity, and I have been astounded at the number of parents who know nothing about this topic and want to know more about it. There are three primary means by which kids process or learn new information:

- visually (seeing the information)

- auditorily (hearing the information)

- kinesthetically (touching or participating).

Knowing your child's preferred way of learning can help her learn more effectively, can improve communication between you and your child, and can assist with her development.

Prior to presenting at a team retreat in Bowral, I was chatting to a father of two children, aged four and one, about the different learning styles people possess and how they related to children. I relayed some of what I'd learned from the International Alliance for Learning (IAL) in the United States. IAL focuses on giving information through schools and corporate training sessions. It encourages people to recognise how others process information and then communicate to them in the best way possible for them to understand it. I explained to this dad that some parents never really understand whether their child primarily processes information by seeing it, by hearing it or by doing.

...some parents never really understand whether their child primarily processes information by seeing it, by hearing it or by doing.

I recalled being at a parent–teacher night for Charley where the teacher said Charley really liked craft time. I asked whether Charley enjoyed the 'doing' part of the craft or whether it was more about what she saw. The teacher acknowledged that she hadn't thought about it in that way, and then answered that it was more to do with what Charley saw. My daughter needs to see what the outcome will look like before she starts working on the task. It needs to be the right colours, sparkly and visually stimulating. Whenever you ask Charley an open-ended question she immediately looks up to the sky or stares straight through you. These are the traits of someone who is a visual learner. Consequently, when you're trying to communicate with a child who is a visual learner, you need to actually show what you mean and have the child look you in the eye.

As I spoke about this to the dad I could almost see the penny drop. He said with his children one could simply be told what needed to happen, but he could tell the other one something a million times and it simply wouldn't go in. He realised that his daughter needed to see what dad was talking about and couldn't simply be told. Once you know this as a parent it makes it a lot easier to communicate with your children.

It's surprising how few people think about this. It's also an issue in the workplace where people constantly communicate over the telephone yet only a small number actually process information by hearing it. Most people need to see it or learn by doing. We wonder why there's such a lack of understanding in the workplace and our homes when we talk to each other, yet for the most part our communication is not even eye to eye. Let's take a look at each style.

'I've told you a thousand times': the learning modalities

Do the words 'I've told you a thousand times' sound familiar? 'Michael, please clean your teeth properly. I've told you a thousand times how to do it—why aren't you doing it?' Parents all over the world wonder why their kids don't understand when they give them instructions. It's important to recognise that this may not be intentional—they simply may not process information well by hearing it.

The primary means that children use to learn new information (just in the same way that you and I would) is in a visual, an auditory or a kinesthetic manner. (There are actually five learning styles if you include olefactory and gustatory.) Let's explore the three main styles in more detail.

Visual learners

If you're a visual person, you take in new information primarily by seeing it. Visual learners need to see pictures, graphs, diagrams, drawings or graphic designs (usually in colour). They will characteristically sit forward in their chairs and appear organised, neat and well groomed. You can tell visual people from the way they talk. Visual people say things such as, 'Show me', 'Let me see', 'I can't see what you mean' and 'Paint me a picture'. When you speak to them, and they are thinking about and processing new information, they tend to look up towards the sky or appear to go into a dream-like state and look straight through you. Generally, about 45 per cent to 55 per cent of all individuals are primarily visual learners.

Auditory learners

Auditory learners need to 'hear it'—that is, they need to have things explained orally. They love music and conversation, are big on tempo, sound, beat and rhythm. Auditory learners say things such as 'That rings a bell', 'It doesn't sound right', 'Talk me through it' and 'Listen to this'. When thinking or processing new information they tend to look sideways as they try to hear the answer to your question. Easily distracted by noise, they typically talk to themselves while learning something new. Interestingly, although the education system is skewed towards auditory learners, only 10 per cent to 12 per cent of any classroom (or boardroom for that matter) will be primarily auditory learners.

Kinesthetic learners

The third learning modality is kinesthetic. These are the touchy-feely people; they want to actually do whatever is being discussed or learned, and like to touch things, play with things or throw things around to learn about them. When they shake your hand they want to hold on for a little bit longer. They like to pat you on the back or give you a hug. They memorise by doing or walking through things. Kinesthetic learners say things such as 'Let me throw it around', 'It doesn't feel right', 'I can't put my finger on it' and 'Just give me some time to wrestle with this'. When you talk to them and ask an open-ended question, they tend to look down towards their feet. They need time to ponder. They find it difficult to give a quick answer as they need to see if it feels right and to do this they need time to process it. In any given room about 35 per cent to 40 per cent of the people in it are primarily kinesthetic learners.

Recognising your child's learning style

How do you work out which learning style your child prefers? Well, when you are doing something with your child, such as teaching him how to clean his teeth, think about how he best processes information. Quite often parents don't look for the cues. Take some time to consider the following questions:

▫ Does your little one love music?

▫ Can she sit for hours while you read her stories and not even look at the book?

▫ Does she love interacting and having a conversation, and does she read or talk aloud to herself?

▫ Does she love picture books and bright colours, and have her room full of pictures, stickers and drawings?

▫ Is your child's appearance very important to her?

Visual children are very caught up with their look. When they look in the mirror they have to look just right. Kinesthetic children are less interested in their appearance—what's more important is that the clothes feel right. They also want to play more, to move around and touch things. They won't be as interested in sitting around reading books and talking.

Look for the signs with your children—this will have a big impact on how you relate to them and impart new information to them. Spend some time looking, listening and watching your kids to pick up on their modalities. For example, if little Tina is a kinesthetic learner, she will want to do it herself. She will want to take control and do it over and over again until she gets it right. Kinesthetic people are notorious for not getting a task done straightaway, but exploring and experimenting until they eventually get it right. This can frustrate visual people who are inclined to say, 'Show me how to do it so I can take care of it as quickly as possible'.

> *Spend some time looking, listening and watching your kids to pick up on their modalities.*

I believe the learning modalities are an important concept for parents to consider, because once you know how your child processes new information and learns, it's much easier for you to impart new knowledge or to discipline your child. If your little one is a visual learner, you need to show him how to do things. Use language such as, 'Let me show you', 'Can you see what I mean?', 'How does this look?' Use lots of colours, pictures and drawings. If your child is an auditory learner, she'll love music and talking. You'll need to use lots of musical-based things. Remember, these are not behavioural traits, they are learning traits. This is the way we all take in new information and learn.

For example, if you were going to a barbecue and you didn't know how to get there, would you want me to draw you a map with visual references such as landmarks? Would you prefer me to call you and tell you how to get there? Or would you prefer that I give you some general directions and you'll just head off and feel your way and eventually get there? This information can also save marriages!

Let's consider another example. A couple are engaged to be married. The bride-to-be is a kinesthetic learner and so wants to take time to look at lots of invitations, feel the stock and the envelopes, and just enjoy the experience of what 'feels' right and makes her comfortable. The groom-to-be is a visual learner. He wants to see the lists, see what looks good or bad, make a decision and move on. You can imagine how this could have ended. What did they do? The bride-to-be spent weeks, if not months, going through all the options—playing with combinations, visiting different stores and enjoying the experience. She finally came up with three different combinations, took them home and laid them out on the dining-room table. The groom-to-be walked in, looked at them all, chose the one he liked the best and everyone was happy. Simply having an insight into how your partner or work colleague operates makes an incredible difference to the entire decision-making process.

It's the same with children. Taking the time to work out whether your kids are visual, auditory or kinesthetic learners will have a bearing on both the classroom experience and the home environment. A father spoke to me not long ago about his son. This dad would come home at night with books about soccer for his son, who was a good soccer player and loved his sport. However, when the dad went into his son's bedroom he would see the books under his bed. Although his son loved soccer and was very happy with the books, he never read them because his learning style was kinesthetic. His son got more benefit and more kicks (so to speak) by going to the park and spending hours kicking the ball with his dad. To learn new information he needed to do it and experiment with it over and over again, rather than read about it.

It's important to note that we can use all three modalities at any given time to process information. We will, however, always favour one. When we're given new information, such as learning how to use a new computer, some people will want to go to the box and start to play with it, others will put it down and ask someone to tell them how to use it, and some will want to be shown how to use it. Personally, I like to be shown. If you show me and tell me I'll learn much faster than if I unpack the box and play with it (this takes too long and is too hard), or if I'm just told how to use it. So don't think your child will be limited to just the one learning style. Every child will want to see, hear and touch things, but generally they will favour one over the others.

Nature versus nurture

There is continuing debate about how much of our development is based on nature and how much is related to nurture. You may be wondering whether everything I've outlined here is to do with nurture or whether it is something to do with nature. Generally, it's a fifty–fifty split. However, it's interesting that some children who love music come from musical families. From an early age they're immersed in the auditory learning style. Yet there are families where the parents are musical, but the child is more of a visual learner, tending towards the arts. In other families one or both parents are into sports, and the child decides to be a mechanic and spend all his time working on the engine of a car. There's no rhyme or reason to the way we learn. The most important thing is that you're aware of the different learning modalities and that you foster them. This will help you teach more effectively and set the right tone for behaviour.

Communication

Once you know your child's preferred learning style you can better communicate with him. Unfortunately, many parents don't take the time to do so. The effects of poor communication can be seen in the stories of some well-known individuals.

In an interview in 2005, author, actress and former fitness icon Jane Fonda talked about her autobiography. Fonda didn't write her autobiography until she was in her sixties. She said it wasn't until that time that she was able to come to grips with the torment and frustration she had faced as a child. During the interview something she said particularly struck me. She said when your parent doesn't see you, when their eyes don't reflect you back, you feel like you're not good enough, and to be loved you have to be perfect.

A lot of the torment and frustration in Fonda's life came from the fact that she felt she was never good enough in the eyes of her father, Henry Fonda. This had a massive effect on her confidence, self-esteem and self-belief, and was the precursor to some of the health and psychological challenges she faced during her early years and even later on as an adult.

Once you know your child's preferred learning style you can better communicate with him.

Barbra Streisand suffered similarly as a result of her parents' lack of support and encouragement. When Streisand burst onto the scene in the stage performance of *Funny Girl*, she was hailed as the next big thing. When her stepfather finally went to see her perform, he gave her a box of lollies. Twenty years later, those lollies were still sitting on the side of Streisand's bathtub. She finally threw them away when she realised she didn't need anyone else's acceptance or approval. When asked whether she was praised by her mother, Streisand said she was the type of woman who would praise her to other people but never to her personally. She said her mother didn't want her to get a big head. Isn't it amazing how twenty or thirty years later, these superstars still harbour this emotion?

I'm sure there are many similar stories carried around by people from all walks of life. The challenge for us as parents is not to let our children grow up without feeling our love, support, praise and appreciation. Make sure that your children see their reflection in your eyes. Work out how they learn best and communicate with them in that manner. Give praise where praise is due, recognise them as individuals, and give them the love and encouragement they deserve. Don't give them praise for the sake of praise; it should be sincere appreciation and acknowledgement for the efforts they put into every aspect of life.

When you hear the stories that Fonda and Streisand and many other actors, musicians and celebrities recount about their childhood, it makes you appreciate what responsibility we have as parents. The good news is that there is no better time to start than right now. Remember, well done is better than well said.

Crouch down

A mate of my brother is raising a delightful, free-spirited little girl who I'm sure is going to grow up loving every minute of life. When I first spent time with them, something that struck me was that every time he needed to address his daughter, the dad kneeled down so that he was at eye level with her. Even if something happened that the dad was unhappy about, he would still crouch or sit down on the ground, look her directly in the eyes and have a conversation with her at her level. This gave the impression that he was respecting her as an individual. Since then I've used this method of communication with children of all ages and I believe it has a measurable impact on the connection you make with children when you look them in the eye.

In the literature on the subject, the common belief is that kneeling or squatting down next to your child (or any child) is a powerful tool for communicating positively with them. Getting close to children allows you to tune into what they may be thinking or feeling. It also helps them to focus on what you are saying or asking because they can see into your eyes. If you're not close to them or you don't have their attention, there's no need for them to look at you during the conversation.

If you respect your child as an individual, it pays to kneel down or sit on the floor to see him eye to eye. What's more, you'll get a lot more cuddles and a lot more smiles, and it's definitely a better opportunity for you to communicate and share meaning with your child. As soon as I come through the front door when I get home from a trip or from work I crouch down to greet my little girl. In the same way, when she gets home from an outing and comes through the front door, I make sure that I'm seated on the carpet near the door, so she can run in and greet me with a cuddle and tell me face to face and eye to eye about her day.

Give your kids more credit

Our kids really are much more intelligent than we often give them credit for. Recently I had a meeting with Geoff Coombes, the other co-founder of our cycling charity the Tour de Cure. We were at his house and I was about to leave when Geoff realised that his then fourteen-month-old daughter had been playing with the remote control for the television and he couldn't find it. We turned the lounge room upside down but still no remote. Then we asked this brilliant little mind, 'Where did you put the remote? Show daddy where the remote is'. Instantly she pointed to the bookshelf, and lo and behold after searching through the books, there was the remote. A toddler could tell us where she had put the remote, yet Geoff, his wife and I turned the place upside down and couldn't find it! The lesson for me that day was never underestimate the intelligence of your child, no matter what age she is.

...never underestimate the intelligence of your child, no matter what age she is.

I don't think many of us give our kids' intelligence the credit or respect it deserves. Most child psychologists will say that we must respect and appreciate how bright our children are. Many of the points that I talk about in this book are based on the fact that we often don't give our children the credit their intelligence deserves. This not only shows a lack of respect for the child and their growth potential, but in some cases it can also stifle their development because they are not being challenged in the appropriate way through language, actions, behaviours and example.

One simple way to do this is to make your child feel important. Kids love it when they can contribute to the family in little ways. Where possible start introducing some simple jobs around the house or little things they can do on their own to help out. Don't assume that because they're young they can't take on tasks. Obviously, common sense needs to prevail here, but I guarantee you'll be surprised if you start challenging them with little chores. It makes them feel important, they take pride in helping out and it's a big part of their development.

Naturally, the more practice they get doing a chore the better they will get at it and the harder they will try. Make sure the tasks are safe, and help your kids be responsible for the chore. This will build their self-esteem, confidence and many other skills depending on what the task at hand is.

Consequences

As your child gets older you can give her more responsibility and ultimately allow her to take responsibility for her own behaviour. However, with this will also come consequences for that behaviour. This doesn't necessarily mean you have to be the bad guy all the time. If you ask your child to put a piece of fruit in his bag for kindy or a sandwich in the bag to take to the beach and he doesn't do it, remind him that when he's at the beach and he's hungry, there won't be any food and he will go hungry. If he doesn't want to eat his dinner that's fine, but remind him that after bath time there won't be more food until the next morning. Sometimes with all good intention we do so much for our kids that we don't allow them to learn for themselves. What's more, we underestimate their potential for understanding or doing and consequently continue to do it for them.

Providing consequences for unacceptable or dangerous behaviour will allow your kids to take responsibility for their own actions. This will make it easier for you and make your children better individuals. Just make sure that when you tell them what you want them to do you crouch down, look them in the eye, make sure they're listening, watching and feeling what you're saying, and that they have understood the consequences.

I always crouch down, have a conversation and then make sure that I get agreement from Charley. I outline all the options and then say, 'Are we agreed? Yes, okay, it's your choice'. From time to time you'll need to go through tantrums and sometimes you may need to make alterations to your agreement to facilitate a good outcome for mum and dad. However, if you stick to your guns, eventually the message will get through and you'll be surprised at how much they take responsibility for.

Ultimately, we need to respect the fact that kids get it, that they understand. They are a lot more switched on than we give them credit for, and we need to give them the respect they deserve.

Mojo checklist

☐ Do you know your child's preferred learning style?

- Is your child a visual learner? Does he need to see the information?

- Is your child an auditory learner? Does she need to hear the information?

- Is your child a kinesthetic learner? Does he need to touch things to learn about them?

☐ Do you give praise and encouragement, and acknowledge your child's efforts?

☐ Do you crouch down when you talk to your child?

☐ Are you giving your child more credit?

☐ Do you make your kids feel important by giving them little chores to do around the house?

☐ Are you giving them more responsibility for their own behaviour and explaining the consequences of their actions?

Chapter 4

Keep your chin up

Young kids are inquisitive and energetic little things. They need stimulation to grow and learn—and this is where us dads come in. Kids learn best from contact with other people, and in this chapter we take a look at some of the lessons we should be teaching our little ones. We need to be building their confidence, instilling them with a positive attitude and encouraging them in all that they do.

Jim Fannin is one of the leading success coaches in the world, working with and developing champions. Jim and I were speaking on the same program for a global life science company at a resort outside Melbourne and I felt privileged to be able to meet and chat with him. In my journal I wrote down something Jim said while he was speaking. He talked about keeping your chin up. He said, 'When you drop your chin you lose your power'.

This really resonated with me, not only in relation to us as adults, but also in relation to our children. When kids get in trouble, lose confidence or begin to doubt themselves, their chin goes to their chest and they start to sulk. At a certain point in their development we need to teach children to keep their chin up, to stay positive and not lose heart. When you keep your chin up it forces your shoulders back, opens up your chest and you breathe more easily. It brings more confidence and you bring more power to whatever it is that you're doing. It's a great lesson for children because no matter what avenues they pursue in the future, it will be those who have that certain mojo or presence about them when they walk into a room who are the ones walking in with their chin up. It also teaches us that when things are down, don't give up—stay positive and work your way through them.

...we need to teach children to keep their chin up, to stay positive and not lose heart.

Naturally we should also teach our children that things won't always go the way they want them to. However, they will find much better solutions to their challenges, problems or hardships by keeping their chin up and working through the issue with a positive mindset. Keeping your chin up automatically changes your physiology, and that alone can have an enormous impact on the outcomes for you and your children. It's the times we work through hardships that define us as individuals and set aside the champions from the rest. It's these times that separate the outstanding dads from the good dads; that separate those who whinge and moan and wallow in pity from those who take it in their stride, take action and get things done.

Freddie the penguin: rewarding their efforts

In the book *Magnificent Mind at Any Age* by Daniel Amen, the author talks about a trip to the zoo with his child. He tells the story of Freddie, the penguin that on command would go and take a toy from his trainer. Following on from the show, Amen asked the trainer how he got the penguin to perform. The trainer explained that when Freddie does anything like what is expected of him, he is noticed and given a hug and a fish. This is the conditioning that teaches people to have positive habits.

A similar approach has been taken by a child psychologist in the US, who has had success in getting children to try foods they don't want to eat. He starts by saying to the child, 'You don't have to eat this, but if you just put it to your lips you can have a treat for dessert'. If the child does put the food to her lips, he leans across gives her a big smile, congratulates her and touches her arm. This provides an anchor for praise. The following night he does the same thing. By the third night he says, 'Just put this piece in your mouth, you don't have to eat it, just put it in your mouth'. Once again, he leans across, gives the child praise and touches the child's arm.

It's the small steps with consistent acknowledgement, encouragement and reward that move a child into the habits you desire.

He continues this for a period of weeks as he coaxes the child, going further and further into the process of recognition and reward for the action required. Each time the child is rewarded with a little treat for dessert, a big smile, verbal recognition and a touch on the arm. I have actually tried this with Charley and had great success. It takes the pressure off forcing her to eat food she doesn't want to eat. The recognition and praise, and the opportunity to get a treat at the end of the meal, has worked very well in getting Charley to at least try foods that she was initially reticent to even look at.

There's a lot of value in the methods used by Freddie the penguin's trainer and the child psychologist. The process should be fun and it should be a giant celebration when the child puts the food to their mouth. It's the small steps with consistent acknowledgement, encouragement and reward that move a child into the habits you desire. If you are finding it a challenge to get your kids to take on a behaviour that you would like them to adopt, give the recognition–praise–reward method a try.

Tell them what you want, not what you don't want

While lining up to pay for my groceries at the local super-market, a mother came up behind me with her trolley full of groceries. Sitting in the trolley and facing her was her son. After she had unloaded all of her groceries onto the conveyer belt, she helped her son out of the trolley and put him on the floor. She then said to him, 'Don't go running off now'.

On hearing this, the first thing that occurred to me was, 'Running off—that could be fun!' And this is exactly what happens in the minds of children. By telling them what you *don't* want them to do, you plant the seed that they could actually do it. By saying, 'Don't run off', the first thing they think is, 'Running off—I hadn't thought about that, what fun!'

Instead, we're better off saying, 'Stay here with me', or 'Let's stay here together and watch the groceries go through the check-out'. This way you're embedding a positive image into the mind of your little one, rather than planting a seed that could lead to the very action you're trying to avoid.

Positive reinforcement has been talked about a lot in child psychology, and it simply means you need to be mindful of the language you use. Reinforce positives rather than reinforce or suggest negatives. If you'd like your child *not* to do something, then reinforce it by telling him what you would like him to do. It's remarkably simple, yet it's surprising how few parents actually do it. In supermarkets, cafes, shops and parks, parents are always bellowing what they don't want the child to do and reinforcing negatives, rather than giving clear, direct instructions of what they would like the child to do. Tell your kids what you want, not what you don't want.

The answer to their problems

One of the greatest gifts we can give our kids is the ability to problem solve. The success that a child will have throughout the years—from facing exams to working on a lemonade stand, to their first job as a shop assistant, to managing a team of people for a small or large organisation—will come down to their ability to problem solve. Personal fulfilment, desire to give back to the community, financial happiness and self-satisfaction will all come from their ability to problem solve better than the next person. Whether they're working for themselves or somebody else, it's people who have the ability to solve problems and find a different way of approaching something who achieve success.

Problem solving starts from an early age. It's about giving children options. Children need to be taught that they always have options when approaching any situation. The more we can exercise their creative minds in their younger years, the more connections that are built between the left and right parts of the brain. If those connections aren't built, they perish. So how do we create an environment where a child is continually thinking in terms of options and more than one way of doing something?

From the earliest age, when a child starts to put together thoughts, it's worth challenging her to make decisions or think in terms of options. For example, would you like an apple, a pear or a banana? Would you like the strawberry yoghurt, the apricot yoghurt or the blueberry yoghurt? Which vegetable would you like to eat first, the peas, the carrots or the potatoes? Would you like to go to the park, the indoor play centre or the beach? You choose. These types of questions allow children to exercise their creative spirit, weigh up the options and decide what they would like to do.

Children need to be taught that they always have options when approaching any situation.

As well as asking questions of your children, you also need to give them time to think of their answer. Don't answer for them! Many times when an open-ended question is asked of a child and he doesn't answer fast enough, the parent jumps in to either ask another question or answer for them. We need to give children the space to think things through. If they're not quick to answer, perhaps they're still processing it. Who's to say they have to answer in a certain amount of time anyway? Generally, the time we expect a child to have an answer for something or make a decision is a parameter that's imposed by us.

How soon should we start this option building in children's minds? I believe that from the minute a child can sit up and point, she should be given the opportunity to start the process. As I've said before, I truly believe that we underestimate the intellectual ability of children in regards to making decisions about their wants. Put three pieces of fruit on the high chair tray and let the baby choose one. She may not be able to do it, but who's to say that those connections aren't being built in the child's genius mind?

All through life we are required to problem solve. Thankfully, if this wasn't promoted to you in your childhood, it's not too late to learn. In my previous books *Who Stole My Mojo?* and *What Made You Think of That?*, I spoke a lot about creativity and imagination and how it's a learned process. After all, creativity and innovation is simply problem solving at its best! In many ways children are better equipped than you and I to be able to make their own decisions and solve problems—all that needs to be done is to foster that talent.

Be careful what you say

There's no doubt that as parents we need to watch what we say and do because kids will copy us. How many times has a parent let a naughty word slip only to have it repeated back by a child? There are certain words that we can take out of our vocabulary to help foster creativity in our children.

My daughter, Charley, has been vocalising from an early age, jabbering on and trying to string words together. Maybe it's because my wife and I had done so much reading and talking to her that she took it upon herself to try to verbally communicate with us. Sometime after Charley started vocalising, my wife, Emanda, was at her mothers' group and some of the women began to compare the feats of their children. Some kids were walking early, some were running, some could draw really well and some had other attributes that their mother thought was wonderful. One of the mothers commented on Charley's 'talking'. Emanda said that Charley had been doing it for quite a while and it was just something that she had picked up. The mothers in the group responded by saying, 'I bet she knows the word "no"!'

When Emanda came home and told me the story I was horrified! I couldn't believe that the first word a mothers' group would think a child would learn was 'no'. What sort of framework are you setting up for a child if the word they learn is 'no'? Unfortunately this is the norm in many households. We have intentionally never used the word 'no' with Charley, instead finding other ways of letting her know that something is not ideal. It's a great challenge to keep finding new and interesting ways to get the message across to teach Charley right from wrong and safe from unsafe, but it is also important to us to foster her creative spirit and not create barriers or ceilings over her thinking.

When you are with your children or you are near a playground, listen to the language that mums and dads are using with their kids and think about how easy it is for us to create ceilings over our children's ability simply through vocabulary. The language we use can very quickly put a bucket of water over the little spark growing within our child. Check and edit your own language and make sure that it is nurturing, encouraging and motivating, rather than restrictive and hindering.

It's okay for kids to fail

American entrepreneur Sara Blakely is the creator of a shapewear brand called Spanx. Sara realised that there was something missing in the women's lingerie category and so, from a back room in her home, she set about creating a product to fill that gap. What Sara has done is both inspirational and a great example of the power of imagination.

During a keynote speech, Sara said that in her childhood her dad would sit at the dinner table and ask both her and her brother what they had failed at that week. If they said they had failed at nothing, he would be disappointed. You see, Sara's dad knew that if you're not failing it means you're not trying new things. If you're not failing, you're not risking anything and if you're not failing, you're not pushing yourself out of your comfort zone.

For many parents, if a child fails at something they automatically believe that it is not a good thing and are disappointed. Sara's father, on the other hand, spun that approach around by encouraging his children to step outside the norm, try new things and risk failure. What a mindset to create in children! And the proof is in the pudding.

Another example of support from a father was told by actor Sharon Stone in an interview. When Sharon was at high school she received a report that was full of her bad behaviour and she was called to the principal's office with her father. The principal went through the report and it seemed to Sharon that she was about to get in trouble. Her father sternly asked her, 'Did you do this?' Sharon replied, 'Yes', and his response was, 'Good, keep doing it'. He then turned to the principal and said, 'Never hold my daughter back'. Sharon said she realised that it's not a matter of how good or bad or up or down you are, it's about your level of commitment. If you get in there and give it all, the audience will love you because you had the guts to do it. This philosophy was passed down to Sharon from her dad. There's no reason we can't take these lessons and apply them to our own children and develop our own philosophies.

...if you're not failing, you're not pushing yourself out of your comfort zone.

Children need to fail. They need to feel sad, anxious and angry to help them learn the skills of recovery, moving on and keeping their chin up. When they encounter hardships and we try to alleviate those hardships for them, so that they don't experience failure and things not going their way, we make it harder for them to learn to deal with disappointment and move on. The result is that we weaken their self-esteem, as they won't have the confidence to deal with hardships or to find a new path and solutions.

By not letting children understand what it's like to feel bad, it makes it harder for them to understand what it's like to feel good and experience being in the moment. This is all part of teaching them persistence, which is surely one of the great values that children can take with them and that will put them ahead of the pack.

Building confidence

Not long ago I was having lunch with a close friend of mine and we were discussing our children. He was talking about his daughter who had just started school. He said she had been going for a few of weeks and in the last week had written her first sentence. Naturally it was quite an achievement and everyone was very excited. No-one could read the sentence, but that wasn't important. What was important was that it made sense to the little girl and to her teacher. The teacher was excited because she said that for children, having the confidence to write and show off their first sentence was the starting point, and from there the floodgates open and their ability develops very quickly. She said the hardest part for most children was actually writing the first sentence, knowing that one of the parents or teachers would then critique it.

In my work I see it all the time, when people in an audience are motivated and challenged to think differently.

During a session, when they apply this thinking to a particular issue and find an interesting or different way of doing something, they get the confidence to do it again. Often what people lack is the confidence to start or the confidence to speak up. Once they understand how their thinking works, they can start to demonstrate to themselves and others how thinking differently can start a procession of wonderful, fresh new ways of approaching the everyday.

I can't help but think that many such secrets lie with our children, yet we're constantly correcting them, telling them how things should be done and putting them into a box. We need to listen to our children rather than automatically telling them what to do. In doing so, not only will we be helping to build their confidence, we are likely to learn some valuable lessons from our little ones.

The mimic

Each month Charley and I go to the zoo; we have done since she was one year old. It's a great outing and something I always look forward to. We're Zoo Friends, which means we can come and go from the zoo as much as we want. I like to get to the zoo right on opening time because there are fewer people and in most cases the animals are being fed, so you're able to get up close and watch.

There's a great book called *Reclaiming Childhood* by William Crain. The author's view is that nature plays a huge part in a child's learning and development. He argues that children are particularly drawn to nature and benefit from rich contact with it. Also that the modern child's isolation from nature contributes to some common emotional problems. This book is an interesting read and reinforces how important it is for children to play in gardens and parks, and to visit the zoo to see animals and nature in the best natural surroundings possible.

...much of what we do and how we act will be mimicked in some way by our children.

One morning at the zoo Charley and I were walking towards the gates and I happened to glance at my watch and at the same time I noticed that Charley, who was in my arms, started glancing at her wrist. It made me realise how much children mimic their parents. We need to be very careful in what we do because children learn mostly from observation.

In the controversial book *The Nurture Assumption* by Judith Rich Harris, the author discusses how three- or four-year-old children use the direction of a person's gaze and the expression on their face as an indication of what is going on inside that person's mind. She says that children's mind-reading abilities have been taken for granted, so it is only recently that these developments have been noticed.

The same is true of children's mimicking. Parents who are constantly rushing around, stressed and doing four things at once will be mimicked. The dad who comes home at night, grunts at his children and spends the next hour on his laptop or mobile phone pacing up and down the lounge room will be copied. The eating habits of parents who have an unhealthy diet will also be copied by their children. We need to be aware that much of what we do and how we act will be mimicked in some way by our children.

When Charley was two and a half we went for one of our visits to the zoo. It was during the school holiday period and as such the place was full of mums and dads with their kids checking out the animals. It was a wonderful atmosphere. Before we got there Charley had decided that the animals she particularly wanted to see were the koalas, the chimpanzees and the gorillas. We went to the chimpanzees first. This was a fantastic time to see them as they were rushing around interacting with each other, grabbing food and climbing up trees. Normally we would only spend about five minutes at each enclosure before Charley would want to move on to the next animal, but on this day she wanted to spend fifteen minutes or more just sitting and watching the chimps. Of course this was great for me as the two of us just sat there, talking and watching the chimps put on a show.

What I noticed was the number of parents who were breezing past the chimps with children being dragged behind them en route to the next animal. I doubt that the kids got a good look at any of the animals. Maybe there was good reason for the rushing, but I was amazed at how most parents were dragging their children by the hand from enclosure to enclosure. I was quite pleased that Charley had taught me this lesson about sitting and enjoying something and not breezing past everything in a blur.

The problem is that hurrying from one place to the next and not taking the time to stop and look around for a while becomes another action that children mimic. It will become the norm for them, and the way they in turn will interact with society. Think about it — do you really want your kids to be like you?

Change your thinking

Over the years I've spoken to many parents who are concerned by the environments that their children are exposed to when mixing with other groups of children at play groups, kindergarten or socially. Sometimes attitudes can be brought home that don't sit in line with the environment that the parents are trying to create.

One dad I knew took an interesting approach with his children who were starting to look on the negative side of life. Each evening he would sit at the dinner table with his daughter and ask a couple of questions. He would ask, 'What did you do really well today?' He then let the child recall all the good things from the day. The next questions he would ask (in no particular order) were: 'What did you really like about today?', 'What are you looking forward to about tomorrow?' and 'What are you going to do and what are the great things that are going to happen for you tomorrow?' These questions are all framed in a very positive and light manner. He said that it takes effort, but commented, 'What in life that's worthwhile doesn't take effort?'

Now, your children may not want to answer all these questions on the first evening and it may take some persistence to break through to them and start this dialogue. Give it a try regardless of whether or not your children are developing negative attitudes. It's a wonderful way to get them to focus not only on the best things from their day, but also on what they are looking forward to tomorrow.

So what are the steps for dads? Be alert to behaviours, beliefs or thinking styles that you feel uncomfortable with. Start to recognise when the kids are exercising this behaviour, belief or thinking style, and challenge it by introducing new ones. Challenge it by asking a series of questions such as those just mentioned. I would also recommend making up your own questions that suit you and your family, and it gives you a chance to be a bit more creative. The next step is to do it over and over and over. The only way to make true change is by reinforcing it continually. It's the repetition that will ingrain it into your little boy or girl. It takes effort, persistence and the right technique. You have all three—you just have to put the time and effort into it.

Please release me

As I mentioned earlier in the book, each year I stage an event called the Day of Inspiration at the Four Seasons

Hotel in Sydney as part of the fundraising for the Tour de Cure cycling foundation. One of the speakers at the 2009 event was David Bussau, an inspiring social entrepreneur. David opted out of the corporate world at the age of thirty-five when he felt as though he'd had enough of living in a world dictated by success, money and possessions, and wanted to do something more with his life. So he moved to the jungles of Thailand for five years so he could understand more about the nature of world poverty.

Being judgemental is one of the greatest ceilings we have in our relationships with our family and our children.

Since then, David has created an organisation called Opportunity International, which provides finance for people in poverty to help them to get a leg up in creating their own commercial enterprise. He believes through this people in poverty can build a quality of life. Opportunity International currently has over $1 billion in loans to people in poverty in countries all over the world and 11 000 staff worldwide. David was awarded the Ernst & Young Australian Entrepreneur of the Year in 2003, the Australian Council for International Development Human Rights Award in 2006, the Beta Gamma Sigma Award for Entrepreneurship in 2007 and was named Senior Australian of the Year in 2008. Talk about an outstanding individual who has achieved outstanding results for a world in poverty!

The reason I speak so highly of David is that not only is he an incredible gentleman who is taking on world poverty and winning, but when asked at the Day of Inspiration what the greatest achievement in his career was thus far, he said being married for forty-four years. He was then asked how he had managed to achieve that success when he was on the road so much. David replied that from day one he and his wife had an agreement to 'release' each other to allow them to be the best they could be. She released him to do what he had to do and in turn he released her to pursue what was important to her. He said by releasing others you allow them to be the person they want to be, deserve to be and have a right to be. He said this has not only contributed to the success of his marriage, it also gave him two wonderful purpose-driven children whom he is extremely proud of.

There is much to think about here for us dads. We need to release our wives or partners to allow them to be the best they can be in whatever they choose to do. This can be hard for a lot of us because we tend to have a perception about how things should be and how others should act, achieve or conduct themselves. We judge others and we have preconceived notions about how things should be done in their world. Being judgemental is one of the greatest ceilings we have in our relationships with our family and our children. David's approach is quite the opposite. Release them, don't judge them and allow them to take on their own purpose.

I admire that David has done what he's done and still has a marriage that he's proud of and two children who are purpose-driven. I can only imagine that having purpose-driven children comes from allowing them the freedom of thought and expression that comes from not prejudging or dictating to them how their life should pan out, but instead giving them the freedom to find their own ambitions and dreams, and take on their own purpose in life.

In fact I would challenge a lot of fathers to think about what their own purpose is. Is your purpose to run a business, to make money, to achieve your budget and profit-and-loss statements for the business? If so, that's not really a purpose, it's just a goal. Most outstanding dads I know have a purpose that goes way beyond how they make money. All of the happiest people I know have a purpose that goes above and beyond just making money or running a business, which are purely a means to an end for them. They've got a greater purpose that they can articulate to you at any given time.

If you are the greatest influence on and a hero to your children, which I suspect you are, then this is another instance where you lead by example. Once you find a purpose it will reflect in your personality, your physiology, your beliefs, your language and ultimately the image reflected back in the eyes of your children.

Write down what your purpose is on the notes pages at the back of this book. If you are unable to write down your personal purpose in life right now, then I suspect you don't really have one and you should make it a mission to find one.

Calling home

I remember being at a conference one night and hearing another dad next to me talking to his son whom he had called in the break. Although I couldn't hear the other end of the phone call, his conversation went like this: 'How was your day today? Did you have fun? Were you a good boy? Are you going to bed now? All right, that's great, put your mother back on'. You can imagine that the boy on the other end was answering, 'Yep, yep, yep, yep' to all the questions before saying goodnight to his dad. This was not much of a conversation and it did not extract any worthwhile information from the child. Yet this dad would have walked back inside thinking that he'd done the right thing and had a conversation with probably the most important person in his life along with his wife. Closed questions give you a closed response and that's not a conversation. It's one person talking to another person and getting nothing back.

Conversely, when I was touring overseas with another speaker, each evening I would hear him on the phone to his children. His conversation went like this: 'What did you do at school today? Tell me about that. What was the best part of your day? What have you guys got planned for tomorrow? What are you looking forward to? What are you going to do tonight before you go to sleep?' These are all open-ended questions. This dad promoted a true conversation between himself and his daughters. Not only did he learn something about their day, but I believe he also made them feel like he was genuinely interested in their lives. His conversations would go for ten minutes, whereas the first dad's conversation went for ten seconds. One makes the child think about their response and enhances their creativity and the other doesn't. One gives you a true connection with the person on the other end of the phone and one doesn't. This of course begs the question, which dad are you?

I'm not saying this is easy—it does take some effort to think of open-ended questions and frame them in such a way as to get your kids to open up and talk. It may be a little difficult at first if they're used to closed questions, but it's up to you to set the standard and put the effort in to create a true dialogue with your children.

Winners and ...

Every dad wants their child to be a winner. Throughout their lives, children are asked to compete. Whether it's being marked in an exam, applying for a job, on the soccer field or through university results, our children are benchmarked against each other whether we like it or not. We've all been brought up to know that there are winners and losers. Our children are going to have to learn that it's very hard to win all the time and, unfortunately, if they don't cross the line first, the automatic reaction of society is to say that you are a loser—you lost the match.

The International Alliance for Learning (IAL) in the US has an interesting approach to this. Once when I was presenting a session at the IAL, I sat in on another presenter's session after mine had finished. During his speech he said to the audience, 'Of course there are winners and there are...' Almost in chorus, the entire audience said, 'Losers!' He said, 'No, there are winners and there are learners'. Our children are going to be asked to compete in a lot of aspects of their lives, but the important thing that we can take from this as parents is to teach our children from the youngest age that there are winners and there are learners. That is, if you don't achieve what you set out to achieve in a competition, learn from it and use that to better yourself next time.

The true challenge for our children is to set their own standards and compete with themselves.

Our kids need to know that the only person they should be competing against is themselves. Perhaps designer Karl Lagerfeld said it best when he described his motto for life: never compete, never compare. If you encourage your children to not compete against or compare themselves with others, then you are setting them up for a life of learning. The real challenge for our children is to set their own standards and compete with themselves. If a child doesn't win a game or succeed in topping the class, the most important question for her to ask herself is whether she did her personal best. If she didn't, what can she learn from it? When you compete against and compare yourself with others you take your eye off your own performance, and that means you're not concentrating on the most important thing of all — doing and being your best.

During the 2009 Tour de France, British cyclist Mark Cavendish was winning the sprint finishes of the tour. An interviewer asked Mark who he thought his greatest opponent for the sprinter's green jersey was. Mark replied that he didn't know and he didn't care. He said the more time he spent thinking and worrying about other people, the less time he focused on the most important thing—getting to the finish line first. This is why Mark is considered to be the world's greatest sprint finisher in road racing.

You have to admire that his focus is solely on being the fastest sprinter in the world and getting to the finishing line first. He focuses on doing the best he possibly can for him and his team. If we can instil this type of thinking in our children, it will help them enormously in the future. If they do all the right things, focus on their own performance and don't achieve what they had set out to achieve, then the important thing is for them to identify what they learned.

Mojo checklist

- ▫ Are you encouraging your kids to keep their chin up and stay positive?

- ▫ Do you use the recognition–praise–treat method when you want your kids to adopt a new behaviour?

- ▫ Are you telling your kids what you want, rather than what you don't want?

◻ Are you being patient and giving your kids a chance to figure things out for themselves, rather than jumping in to solve the problem for them?

◻ Are you watching the language you use and setting a good example, so your kids pick up good habits?

◻ Do you encourage your kids to try new things and risk failure?

◻ Are you challenging their thinking and helping them develop a positive attitude by asking them questions that focus on the good things in their day?

◻ Do you know what your purpose is?

◻ Do you ask your kids open-ended questions to have real conversations with them?

◻ Do you encourage your kids not to compare themselves with others, but to set their own standards and compete with themselves?

Chapter 5

That's not a face: unlocking the creative spirit

One major consideration for us as parents is how we foster creativity and imagination in our children. Bestselling author Carl Honoré summed it up perfectly in his book *Under Pressure*. He said that the biggest rewards in the future will go not to the 'yes' people who know how to serve up an oven-ready answer, but to the creatives—the nimble-minded innovators who can think across disciplines, delve into a problem and relish the challenge of learning throughout their lives. These are the people who will come up with the next Google, invent an alternative fuel or develop a plan to end poverty in Africa. Our job is to stoke the imaginative fire in our children—and, as I've said before, we do this through play and curiosity.

I often hear parents getting frustrated at their children who are continually firing questions at them. Yet this is the very essence of curiosity. It's the child who asks questions and explores possibilities, constantly pushing for new options, who will make his way into the future creating a path of imagination that leads to the next Google or YouTube. It's only those children who have a curious mind, who ask, 'Why not?', 'What if?', 'How could we?' and challenge for a different way to do things who will unlock the future for themselves and our society.

Albert Einstein spelled it out even more clearly when he said to stimulate creativity one must develop a childlike inclination to play and a desire for recognition. When it comes to what children should be doing in their early years, play is far more important than chasing milestones. This is contrary to what we are taught or pressured to deliver through society. Play is a loaded word these days. In our workaholic, get-ahead culture, play can seem like a guilty pleasure or an excuse for wasting time—it's not. Let your kids play and unleash their creativity.

What do you think?

As parents we are often bombarded with 'why' questions. Why this, why that, over and over again. It can become tedious, annoying and drive us to dismiss these questions with a quick, 'Because I said so!' This response obviously doesn't foster a child's creative spirit, but understandably can be given due to frustration. Our children's natural curiosity is driven by questioning. Quite often their 'why' questions are just repetition and a force of habit where they're not actually doing any thinking for themselves. Here's one tip worth packing into every parent's kitbag: when your child asks why, say, 'I'm not sure, what do you think?' or 'Hmmm, that's interesting, what do you think?' What this does is put the question back on to the child, thereby encouraging her to do some thinking and ponder the issue herself.

...when faced with a child constantly asking you 'why' questions, throw it back to him and ask what he thinks.

I've used this myself a number of times and had some very interesting responses. Sometimes when I've thrown this back to children I've been playing with, their eyes look up to the sky and they start to imagine what an answer might be. More often than not these little geniuses know the answer, they just haven't taken the time or effort to think about it themselves. Sounds familiar in the corporate world too, doesn't it?

So when faced with a child constantly asking you 'why' questions, throw it back to him and ask what he thinks. This also leads to a real discussion between you and the child about all the potential answers that might go with the question. One of the greatest things we can teach our kids is to be thinkers. You do this by posing questions that they can ponder for themselves.

If you ask your child what she thinks and she says 'I don't know', here's a terrific response: 'Yes, honey, I know you don't know, but if you did know, what do you think it might be?' This automatically takes the pressure off them to have to know the answer and they can then take a stab in the dark and say anything they want, because, first, you're giving them time and space to think, and, second, they are allowed to say whatever they think. This is a wonderful trick for drawing out curiosity and imagination in your children. Be persistent and curiosity will shine through.

Children's drawings

In *Reclaiming Childhood* by William Crain, the author provides an interesting premise for readers to consider. He comments that children below the age of eight love to express their creativity—through singing, dancing, drawing, stories and roleplaying. It is through these activities that their talents blossom. Many psychologists are now making reference to the fact that, sadly, parents are stealing childhood away from their kids. When a child draws a face or writes a song, if it doesn't match the way the face or song should be in the mind of the parent, the parent automatically corrects the child or, worse still, some parents take the pen and redraw it for the child.

This is taking away imagination and creativity from our children. We're taking the creation they see in their own mind and forming it into an image that we believe is how things should be as governed by society. I see it happen all the time. When a child draws a cat it's just a series of circles with no particular shape to it. The parent then takes the crayon and draws the cat the way it should be. But who is to say the way the child has drawn the picture is not another way to draw a cat?

The more we correct children in the area of creativity and imagination, the more we build walls and ceilings around their thinking. This is not to say that children shouldn't know the difference between acceptable and unacceptable behaviour at the dinner table or around other children. It also doesn't mean children shouldn't know the difference between right and wrong in terms of safety and areas that could harm them. This is purely to do with creativity and imagination and the areas of dance, drawing, poetry and make believe that children delve into in their first five to seven years.

Pablo Picasso was heard to have said, 'Once I drew like Raphael, but it has taken me a whole lifetime to learn to draw like children'. Children don't have barriers. They don't know how things are supposed to be. They just create the way they see things and don't really care about how society sees things. Children don't draw because it's right or wrong, they just draw. Instead of thinking about our own goals as parents, we should consider the child's interests and the child's needs. We should allow children to create the way that they wish to create. We have a responsibility to foster and help grow their imagination. We have a responsibility to help their fantasies flourish and it will pay off in spades as they get older.

Be patient

One Christmas I was at a family get-together with grandparents, parents and children, and it was time to unwrap the presents. As is family tradition, it's one present at a time and everybody watches you unwrap it. One of the kids was given a present that was a decent size and as the child started to attack the present, she was having trouble getting the wrapping off. Quick as a flash, one of the parents moved the child aside and said, 'Let me help', and proceeded to unwrap the present. You could see the disappointment in the child's eyes as the joy and intrigue of unwrapping a present was taken away. This was done obviously for a couple of reasons. Either the parents were on a schedule and didn't have time for the child to take so long, or they didn't appreciate that the unwrapping was just as much a reward as the present itself.

Parents tend to jump in too quickly to do things for their children.

Parents tend to jump in too quickly to do things for their children. Something as simple as unwrapping a present should not be considered a frustration or a time waster. Kids should be able to take as long as they want, unless they get to a point where they are frustrated and it starts to detract from the pleasure of the exploration. At this point the assistance should be minimal, just enough to start the unwrapping, so the child can continue ripping and tearing to get to the prize.

When we do it for them, we are short-circuiting the process and teaching them that when they start to struggle, it's time to get someone else to solve the problem. This will shorten the amount of time that a child will spend on a problem, therefore limiting his creativity. As well, with parents always solving the problem, we lessen the curiosity and play that a child can experience. We've all been frustrated when a child spends more time playing with the wrapping than they do with the actual present. This is because kids don't judge, they just do what they enjoy and often that's not the present itself, it's all about the wrapping.

Curiosity in play

One of the books that has had the most profound effect on me as a parent is *Einstein Never Used Flash Cards* by Kathy Hirsch-Pasek and Roberta Michnick Golinkoff. The premise of the book is that multibillion-dollar corporations are being built around flash cards, learning devices, educational games and toys to help children become intelligent and make the grade. Parents are feeling pressured to have their child meet the standards of Mr and Mrs Jones and their child next door, and to reach the appropriate academic levels to go into the best schools and universities.

This book builds on the idea that children with loving parents who enjoy them, play with them and offer guidance and suggestions as they explore their environment will be healthy, emotionally well adjusted and psychologically advanced. The authors argue that you don't need to spend your hard-earned dollars to educate your babies to make the grade. Simply, play is to early childhood what petrol is to a car — it is the very fuel of every intellectual activity that our children engage in.

This is truly a wonderful book and a must-read, in my opinion, for any parent with a child under the age of seven. The foundation of this book is that it has been proven scientifically that children are born with everything they need to create. Our job is to build an environment around them to allow them to flourish. A child's brain is always growing and in the first five to seven years we need to provide the stimulation for them to help that brain shape. It's now a common belief that this environment is created through love, care, play and curiosity.

The question is, do you truly play with your children or do you simply sit in the same room with them while they play? Do you let your children play by themselves doing whatever they like to do with their own toys, drawings and scribbles or do you believe that they must be doing activities to take them towards academic success? Do you promote and foster their curiosity or do you constantly correct them and build ceilings over their thinking? Children are little sponges, and to keep them that way we must avoid drying up their curiosity. We need to be encouraging and not critical. In the areas of creativity, innovation and imagination, we don't always have to be right. Remember, they are little human beings and they may just see things differently from us.

Researchers have discovered that play is related to greater creativity and imagination and an even a higher reading level and IQ scores. Based on the anecdotal research and the evidence that has been collected by psychologists in the area of child development, they believe the new equation is: play equals learning. This premise is backed up for big kids like you and me by the International Alliance for Learning, which believes 'if the body don't move, the brain don't groove'. What this means is that to have a true learning environment, whether it's for big kids or little kids, we need to move, interact and play to truly embed new learning.

...some people think that play is a waste of time, but nothing could be further from the truth.

This thinking is not new. Einstein knew the value of play all along when he said, 'Combinatory play seems to be the essential feature in productive thought, before there is any connection with logical construction in words or other kinds of sign, which can be communicated to others'. In modern society, some people think that play is a waste of time, but nothing could be further from the truth.

The problem with over-scheduling

Earlier I mentioned a book by Carl Honoré called *Under Pressure*. It is about the pressure we are putting on children to perform and make the grade. One of the main points from this book is that we over-schedule our children with piano lessons, soccer training, swimming lessons, dance classes, karate and other extracurricular activities. The result is that children, like adults, are left with no time for reflection. When everything is tightly scheduled kids don't learn how to come up with their own ideas or make their own entertainment. In the same way, when we spend eight hours a day in meetings, before returning to our desk to start checking emails, we're leaving no time for creativity. We're getting the job done without any true reflection or productive thinking time.

Honoré reports that in a kidshealth.org survey 41 per cent of children aged nine to thirteen said they felt stressed most or all of the time because they had too much to do and nearly 80 per cent said they wished they had more free time. For children to develop their creativity and imagination they need to have unscheduled time—time to just be. In the US, Harvard University is urging incoming students to check their over-scheduling ways in at the door. On the university's website is an open letter from Harry Lewis, a former dean of the undergraduate school, titled, 'Slow down: getting more out of Harvard by doing less'.

Honoré also notes that studies in many countries have shown that children who eat regular family meals are more likely to do well at school, enjoy good mental health and eat nutritious food. They're also less unlikely to engage in underage sex or use alcohol and drugs. When Steven Spielberg was interviewed about his career and where he had come up with the ideas for his award-winning multibillion-dollar films, he said, 'At the dinner table'. Think about that — Steven Spielberg has seven children and all the ideas for his movies come from the dinner table.

Making sure your kids have unscheduled time and sitting down for a family meal aren't hard to do, but often the most fundamental things are the hardest to put into practice in your world. Neverthless, if you're serious about giving your children the best start in life and developing their creativity and imagination, you'll take these things to heart and try to incorporate them into your day.

Take a leaf from the Montessori style of teaching and observe your children to see where their interests lie. Watch them in play when they are not looking and see what their true interests and desires are. Once you have identified these things, apply your own curiosity and show genuine interest in that passion.

You don't need flash cards, learning tools, games and the latest gadgets to help your children be the best they can be. Children are born with everything they need to be successful. All you need to do is to foster their curiosity and allow them to play.

What we really need is to take the pressure off children and give them the time, space and freedom to be kids again. More importantly, we need to let them hang out, be bored, relax, make mistakes, dream and have fun. While many parents think their children must be stimulated at all times and must be constantly learning, and any down time they have is wasted time, for children less is more. Reflection is an important part of a child's world. It's the reflecting and looking back that builds the memory muscles in children's brains. It's during these times that the greatest creativity and curiosity are born.

...we need to let them hang out, be bored, relax, make mistakes, dream and have fun.

This can be quite challenging if you have just the one child. Often, when your young one is not at kindy or preschool, *you* are her playmate. I know parents who have a designated one-hour period around midday each day for quiet time. During this time the child must retreat to her own room and spend sixty minutes amusing herself. They don't actually have to be quiet, it's more their own personal time and space where they entertain themselves with reading, writing, playing, painting, talking or sleeping. This also gives mum or dad some freedom to take care of their own business or even just relax. This is a good way to reinforce a behaviour that allows a guaranteed down time for both the child and the parents. The discipline and routine of this time out are good to reinforce at a young age, so, hopefully, they take it through into their later years.

Goodness knows that many mums and dads in the workforce could also do with designating some time in their day to sit, think and reflect. Indeed, one of the biggest issues facing most corporates is that they don't have any down time. We all need our own time and space. When one of the coffee brands conducted a survey on the lifestyles of young mums, it was discovered that the thing mums craved above any other prize the brand could offer was some quiet 'me' time — time to sit with a magazine and just be.

Sweets

A woman takes her young daughter to see Gandhi. After lining up for many hours they finally get to see him. The mother asks Gandhi to tell her daughter to stop eating sugar. She tells him her daughter eats sweets and she would like him to convince her that she should stop. Gandhi looks at the mother and says, 'Come back in three weeks'. The woman takes her daughter away and returns three weeks later. After waiting in line again for hours the woman and her daughter finally stand in front of Gandhi. Gandhi looks at the little girl and says, 'Stop eating sugar'. The mother looks at Gandhi and says, 'Is that it?' He nods his head. She says, 'Why didn't you say that three weeks ago. Why did you make us go away and come back and stand in line once again to see you?'

Gandhi replies, 'Because three weeks ago I was still eating sugar'.

There's a lot to be learned from this story. Do an audit on your own personal life to see where you are demonstrating creativity. Are you reading any books? Are you writing or designing? Are you doing interesting work in the garden, interior decorating, reading poetry, playing guitar or learning a language? If you're not doing any of these things, yet your intention is to raise children with a great creative spirit, then you're telling them to not eat sugar when you are eating sugar.

It can be quite a wake-up call to do an audit on yourself, to realise how little you are exercising your own creativity. It's something that needs to be worked on consistently to set the tone and example for your children. Think about it — what are you doing to demonstrate to your children that creativity, imagination and thinking differently are important? Write it down at the back of this book and see how much or how little you are already doing to walk the talk. If you can't make a decent list, then today is the day to make the change.

The lawyer

After I had given a speech to an Adelaide law firm, one of the partners approached me in the break. He had a huge smile on his face as he related a story that had happened to him and his four-year-old stepson. He said each evening he gets home from work and reads his son a bedtime story. Recently he was halfway through the story when the little boy closed the book and said, 'Then what happened, Dad?' His dad froze. He said he was so used to thinking literally about work through the day that when it came to creating a fictitious story to entertain a four year old, he drew a blank.

He said from that point on each day he would close the door to his office for ten minutes and write a story for that night. He now gets a great amount of pleasure from creating a story to tell and what's more, his son loves it. He also felt himself becoming a better problem solver and more creative. He believed that sitting down each day, disconnecting from his life at work and forcing himself to live in an imaginary world and think laterally about a story was exercising his brain and taking him to places he didn't know existed. He said he now looks forward to it and makes it a part of every day.

Reward the effort

In *What Made you Think of That?* I wrote a chapter on leadership in the corporate world, and how leaders unlock the best ideas from the people around them. One of the things I discussed was leaders rewarding the effort of people thinking differently rather than just the idea that comes as a result. In the corporate world, leaders generally only reward the people who have good ideas. They don't reward the effort or process that an individual might go through to find a new way of looking at something regardless of whether the idea comes to fruition or not. However, the juice is in having everyone in the team thinking differently, not just in the ideas that are the outcome.

When you reward effort you are encouraging repetition of that effort. When you only reward ideas, you're not recognising the effort that may have gone into all the ideas that led to that particular winning idea. What gets rewarded gets repeated.

I believe the same should happen with our kids. When kids are given the opportunity to imagine something, they should be rewarded for the effort they put in to that thought. We shouldn't always wait for them to have a great idea to recognise their thinking. Try to catch your child thinking differently and approaching something in a new, imaginative way. Whether he invents a character, rearranges the peas on his plate in an interesting way or simply creates an interesting story for the plush toys he has befriended in his room, reward his thinking and encourage it.

When you reward effort you are encouraging repetition of that effort.

I've heard parents and leaders in the corporate world use language such as 'That's a great idea. I love the way you've approached that', 'That's an interesting angle to take', 'What made you think of that?' and 'That's a very imaginative approach'. Unfortunately, in most households children more often hear negative comments about things they haven't done right or didn't get right. They should be hearing positive language that rewards them for their efforts, particularly in the area of thinking. Remember, what gets rewarded gets repeated!

Create a safe house

During a speech in the UK I met a guy who was keen to share the personal philosophy he had used to raise his children. He said, 'I've always encouraged my children to do whatever they want to do, knowing that if it doesn't work, I'll be there to pick up the pieces'. He went on to relay a story about how his daughter chose a course at university, but after starting it realised it wasn't her passion and not what she really wanted to do. She went to her dad, they talked about it and decided that she shouldn't waste any more time doing it, that she should change courses. This guy had spent the last couple of months working through the issue with his daughter and said she now loves the course she's doing and is doing brilliantly well. This is a lovely philosophy for a dad to have, to support, encourage and help foster a creative spirit in his children.

It reminded me of the speech given by Andrew Stanton, the director of film company Pixar, when he accepted the Oscar for Best Animated Feature in 2009 for *Wall-E*. He thanked Pixar co-founder Steve Jobs for creating a cinematic safe haven. To me, every CEO, senior executive or team leader could take a lesson from that. Imagine if every leader developed a creative safe house in their team, their company or their organisation. This is such a powerful tool. Invariably whenever I work with organisations around the world, one of the biggest barriers to creativity is fear. Steve Jobs, however, is not like other leaders. He believes in thinking differently and challenging the norm. Not only does he live and breathe it, but he also creates a safe house for everyone who works with him.

Every dad should take a lesson from Steve Jobs. Create a safe house for your children where they can explore their creativity, innovation and imagination, and if things don't go well, your children need to know that you'll be there to help and support them. Naturally children need to take responsibility for their own actions and also for fixing things when they run off the rails. However, it's important for children to know that you'll be there for them. After all, when things don't go well, where's the first place that kids go? Back home to see mum and dad.

The guy I met in the UK often repeated his philosophy to his children. This may be something for you to think about—have you or will you create a safe house for creativity for your children?

Mojo checklist

☐ When your kids ask 'why' questions, are you asking them what they think the answer is?

☐ Are you standing back and letting your kids create the way they want to create?

☐ Are you building a home environment, a safe house, in which your kids can play and be creative without constantly being corrected or having their problems solved for them?

☐ Are you playing with your children?

☐ Are you involved in their creative endeavours and a part of their creative, imaginative process to help unlock their great ideas?

☐ Do you allow your kids unscheduled time, time in which they can just be?

☐ Are you setting an example for your kids by exercising your own creativity?

☐ Do you reward your kids for thinking differently?

Chapter 6

Bringing out their best

As dads we have a responsibility to encourage our children to be all that they can be. We have to nurture their talents, help them explore the world and encourage them to learn. Let's take a look at some of the things you can do to get on the path to becoming an outstanding dad and bringing out the best in your children.

Write it down

It amazes me when I'm speaking to audiences how little people write down. So many people seem to believe that they will remember all the key messages, nuggets and shared knowledge that come from spending time listening to your boss, a keynote speaker or a trainer impart knowledge for you and your team. But if you think you're going to remember what has been shared with you past the coffee break, then you are kidding yourself. As I mentioned earlier in the book, only 10 per cent to 12 per cent of any audience are auditory learners. Most of us are visual or kinesthetic learners.

The reason I'm mentioning this now is that there's a lot to remember when it comes to key milestones and learnings, and anecdotes about them. I'm surprised how few parents write down notes about their child's early years. It requires minimal effort to keep a journal next to your bed and every so often write down some key thoughts about your children. Whether it's highlights of what the teacher said at the parent–teacher night, or some funny, quirky comments the kids made that the day, or what their main interests are on a weekly, fortnightly, monthly or yearly basis. What are the passions that your children have in terms of learning, play and development throughout their first five to seven years?

Sir Ken Robinson is the author of a fascinating book called *The Element*. Your 'element' is something that you have a passion for and that you're really good at—in fact, that you excel at. When you can make the element part of your life, you are pretty much doing what you love to do, you're good at it and in most cases you would do it for nothing because you love it that much.

Unfortunately, finding your element is not something taught in schools, and in most cases people go through life without knowing what their element is.

This concept is something I've taken on board and as such I have started to keep a journal of the things that Charley is passionate about. Some of the things I've noted that she loves are books, music, dancing, the water and running. Nothing may come of it, but it's fun to write down some of the key interests or passions that your children have, to see whether they lead to something in their later years.

...it's fun to write down some of the key interests or passions that your children have...

Journaling is good for the soul. It's also a chance for you to take some time out and reflect so that when your child is in her teens and asks you about what she was like growing up, you don't have to sift back through your memory bank, you can actually go to your journal. It shows you have an interest in her. You don't have to rely on your auditory skills, which like most of us would be pretty average, to recall all those things that happened in your child's early years. No doubt some things will register in your mind because you will physically be active with your child during those years, or you'll be able to paint a picture in your mind, but often it's the conversations, the things they say or things you heard that slip your mind that are worth writing down.

Your journal could be a scrapbook, or it could be a file on your computer where you keep a photo or video library of your child growing up. No matter what form it takes, I believe that it's worthwhile making the effort to sit back and record or scrapbook in some way your child's journey. This is not a daily diary, but a list of the passions, interests and things your child excels at from an early age. This is where you and your child discover the element.

Fan the spark

Cus D'Amato was the boxing coach of former boxing world champion Mike Tyson. During the time that Tyson was under the direction of D'Amato, he had the potential to become one of the greatest boxers of all time. As soon as D'Amato died, so too did Tyson's career.

I remember seeing an interview many years ago with Cus D'Amato where he discussed his philosophy of taking troubled boys and turning them into quality men. He spoke about Mike Tyson's difficult childhood and how he saw his job as taking that troubled young kid, giving him some direction and sending him off to a more stable and secure future. He succeeded with Tyson, but unfortunately when D'Amato passed away, Tyson once again lost his direction.

D'Amato's philosophy was to look for a tiny spark within a child and fan it until that spark became a burning ember. He fanned the ember until it became a flame. He then fanned the flame until it became a fire and fanned the fire until it became it became a raging bushfire. He said the challenge was finding the fire within, and then giving it courage, love, structure and discipline until it started to show its true colours. Early on he could see that tiny spark within Mike Tyson.

You can take this lesson in a number of different ways for your own children. As a parent, it's essential to look for that little spark in each of our children. What do they truly love or excel at? Once the spark is found, our job is to give it encouragement, love, structure and discipline to help it grow and become a burning ember. Whatever your kids love, are passionate about and are totally immersed in, encourage them to promote it.

The other spark you can fan in your child is his ability to problem-solve and create options. The greatest spark you can embed in your child's mind is to have him always thinking, 'What else?', 'What else can I do?', 'How can I approach it differently?', 'What else can I add?', 'There's got to be another way to approach this'. If you can create that spark and then fan it to become a burning ember, you have done your job in helping to foster your child's curiosity and imagination. Remember, your little one has everything he needs to grow up to be a genius. Our job is to watch and listen, and when we see that spark, grab the fan.

In some cases we need to help the spark along by providing the flint and a rock. This is done by giving babies and/or toddlers the opportunity to think and select on their own. Constantly challenge them with open-ended questions and give them the space and freedom to answer for themselves. You have to allow them to fail!

The ABCs of food

One Christmas I attended a party at a childcare centre where most of the children were under the age of two. The food that was being served was mostly twisties, chips, M&Ms, cupcakes, jelly snakes and jellybeans. There was one small plate of grapes and another small plate of rice crackers. Needless to say I was horrified! Why would children under the age of two need to know about or acquire a taste for all that junk food? I don't believe that at that age children need to know what sugary, fatty foods taste like or even are. Goodness knows they will be exposed to them quickly enough as they get older, so why start them on a road to obesity at the age of two?

That's not to say that children are not going to want to enjoy a piece of chocolate, a cupcake or a jelly snake in the future, but they should be taught that these are treats and are only for special occasions. There are a couple of reasons for this. First, it's the example that parents give that sets the tone, beliefs and boundaries for children and, second, it's the mindset that you create for your children in their first five to seven years that will carry on for the rest of their life.

Everyone loves treats, but that's exactly what they should be—treats. They should be a reward for achieving something or as a celebration of something. There shouldn't be an expectation that as soon as a child is hungry, he is given rubbish. There shouldn't be an expectation that every time the family goes out the child gets to eat rubbish, or that whenever they pass a hot chip stand or a takeaway food store the child should be allowed to have some. Or that trips to the supermarket mean a fistful of lollies because it is the easiest way to keep the child quiet.

This all comes back to the foundations and beliefs that are set for the child from her earliest age. Associations need to be built in the mind of your little one from the minute she can understand food and choices. In *Einstein Never Used Flash Cards*, the authors talk about how they believe that one hour of educational television programming each day for a child is actually beneficial. *Sesame Street*, *Play School* and the like are good educational programs that can be a reward for your little one who has spent the day running around. There's no reason an association shouldn't be built into the reward of an hour of television, and while doing so she can also enjoy a bowl of fruit. If the association is created early enough, you will find your child will automatically associate the hour of television with eating fruit.

There's no reason an association shouldn't be built into the reward of an hour of television…

The same thing can also apply to dinner. Eat the right foods in the right amounts at dinner and a treat may follow. I know this can be challenging and frustrating for a lot of people. However, it's essential that the boundaries be built in the early years, so you will benefit in the long run. When boundaries aren't built you can see it in the general demeanour, health and mental state of a lot of children and teenagers.

Whether this resonates with you or not, it really comes down to the parameters, barriers and beliefs you have as parents. It's no coincidence that parents who have a strong philosophy and opinion about food and how it can control mood, energy levels and cooperation with children tend to have children who are much more relaxed, attentive, understanding and reasonable. A healthy mind starts with a healthy body.

Get away with your kids

Every couple of months I like to take a trip with Charley for a few days to visit my parents who live interstate. After doing this a couple of times, I really began to understand what a stay-at-home parent goes through every day looking after a child. I can only imagine what it must be like doing it with several children! If you really want to get an understanding of what a stay-at-home parent goes through on a daily basis, then pack up your kids and take a trip away for three or four days. Every food break, toilet break, bath, bed time, bad mood—the whole works—it's all you. It really makes you appreciate your partner that much more.

It does the spirit good to go away for a weekend and be the one to shoulder the burden. It builds an amazing connection particularly when it involves travel and all the associated stresses. Charley and I have been doing this now for a few years and it builds a great bond, makes us better communicators and, what's more, we have a lot of fun! The more you travel with children at a younger age, if you're able to, the better they become at it. So if you have the chance, get on a plane, take a train or get away in the car for the weekend with the kids.

Armageddon

The rock band Aerosmith is unquestionably one of the greatest rock acts of the modern era. Over four decades Aerosmith has consistently packed out stadiums with their live shows, and are admired as a quality rock outfit who know how to put together a great album. However, it wasn't until the song 'I Don't Want to Miss a Thing', written for the soundtrack of the movie *Armageddon*, that Aerosmith actually achieved their first number one single.

I have adopted 'I Don't Want to Miss a Thing' as my theme song for Charley. I know it may sound odd, but because I'm quite a visual and auditory learner, I've found it beneficial to have a song that I can go back to every so often to help me refocus on what is important. Every now and then when I feel as though I'm losing track of my perfect world, I put on 'I Don't Want to Miss a Thing' and it reminds me of my main priority—to be an outstanding dad. Part of my commitment to myself is to be there as my daughter grows up and not be a dad who is always missing in action.

From the minute Emanda and I knew we were going to have a baby I adopted the Aerosmith song to remind me of what the most important thing in the world is—that is, put first things first. I've seen too many of my mates miss out on their children's milestones as they're growing up such as their first steps, their first footy match, their first theatre production or first day of school. I'm not going to be one of those guys and this song is just an anchor that helps refocus me. I have it on my iPod and every so often on my way home from work I put it on. You may have your own visual, auditory or kinesthetic cues, but I wanted to share mine as a powerful way to put first things first.

Part of my commitment to myself is to be there as my daughter grows up...

Take it at their pace

One Friday morning in January 2007 a casually dressed, thirty-something man stood inside a train station in Washington, DC, and began to play the violin. He played for forty-three minutes, and in that time more than 1000 people walked past—or rushed past—on their way to work.

Three minutes went by before someone noticed the musician—a middle-aged man paused, turned his head, and then hurried on. After six minutes someone stopped and listened for a few minutes. From time to time people threw in change as they rushed past.

The only people who really paid much attention to the violinist were the few children who walked past, all being pulled along by their busy parents and all looking back over their shoulder as they were led away.

By the end of the musician's performance only six people had stopped to listen. About twenty people had given him money, but continued on their way. He collected $32.17.

The man at the train station was internationally acc-laimed violinist Joshua Bell. He played one of the most difficult pieces of music ever written, on an instrument worth $3.5 million. His performance was arranged by *The Washington Post* as an experiment in context, perception and priorities. In an ordinary setting at an inconvenient time, would beauty be recognised and appreciated?

If we can't take time out of our lives to stop and listen to an incredible musician play some of the best music ever written, what else are we missing?

This story illustrates how children were intrigued by the talent of the man playing at a train station, but their parents were too busy getting from point A to point B to notice the amazing sounds. Quite often I see the same thing happening when I walk Charley to kindy. Parents have their minds set on getting their child to and from the kindy front door as soon as possible, dragging their children in and out of the car or along the footpath to meet their own deadlines. All along the way the children want to stop and check out a leaf, pick up a stick or look at a light pole with its light still on even though it's eight o'clock in the morning.

It's this interest children have with the smallest things that sparks their curiosity and pays off in creativity as they get older. As we drag them away from these things, we not only increase the cortisol to their brains, we also deprive them of the opportunity to question and develop their curiosity.

When walking with kids, walk at their pace. If they want to stop and look at something, then it should be okay to do so. Now, I know you're sitting there thinking, 'If I did that I'd never get anywhere because every trip to kindy or the shops would take three hours'. That's true and I agree. However, there need to be some walks where you walk at their pace and let their curiosity take over. Ideally, this would be more often than not. On other occasions, for whatever reason, you may have a deadline and if you explain this to your child, he is likely to understand and behave accordingly.

From my experience, there are some days when the household is running late, but rather than rush I explain the need to keep walking directly to kindy and not spend too much time stopping and exploring. Kids get it. We just need to give them credit for understanding by explaining that sometimes we need to move a little more briskly from point A to point B. If this is happening every day as part of your routine — going to and from the shops, kindy, swimming or soccer — then you are depriving your children of creativity.

I included the story of Joshua Bell in my newspaper, *The Espresso*. (Details are at the back of the book; you can subscribe for free.) This story really resonated with parents. I received emails from all over the world commenting on how beautiful it was and how it even emotionally touched some people. So many parents are so obsessed with getting things done that they are depriving their children of the chance to develop their artistic orientation, their ties to nature and other distinctive traits in the early years such as questioning, pondering and exploration.

When walking with kids, walk at their pace.

In the terrific book *Reclaiming Childhood* by William Crain, the author makes reference to the Montessori way of teaching children. He explains that Montessori teachers believe children have an inner wisdom that allows them to know what they need to develop. In their view, Montessori schools allow children to be guided by nature, and teachers follow the children's lead. Crain discusses how in some schools the children actually set the curriculum. For example, a walk through nature is rewarded by children finding the things that intrigue them, and a curriculum is then built around that process. If a group of children find fungi interesting on their nature walk, they will spend the next week learning, understanding and playing with fungi. This is the premise of child-centred learning, but this process can't work if children are being pulled from pillar to post to meet their parents' deadlines.

The other enormous advantage in the Montessori style of teaching is that by allowing children to pursue their own deep interests, they develop their own love of learning. Surely this is one of the greatest traits we can teach our children—to have a love of learning. No matter what venture or area they move into, if they love to learn they are putting themselves light-years ahead in the game of life. Your children will feel happier and more fulfilled, and will likely reach out wanting to learn new things.

Mojo checklist

◻ Are you writing down your child's milestones, the funny things they did or said, and what their passions and interests are?

◻ Are you looking for that spark in your child? If you have found it, are you fanning it?

◻ Are you encouraging healthy eating habits?

◻ Do you have an anchor that helps you refocus on your family?

☐ Are you slowing down and taking things at their pace?

☐ Are you fostering their curiosity by letting them explore?

Chapter 7

Final thoughts

Since beginning the journey of writing *My Dad's Got Mojo*, more than ever I've been alerted to stories told by other dads that refer to their role in the household. These men are tearing their way through the corporate world at the expense of living a fulfilled life in their household or truly engaging with their children. At some point, however, something will happen and they will need to look at the man in the mirror and, hopefully, the penny will drop for them. It is my hope that this book gets you thinking now about your own world, so you won't need to have that conversation with yourself in the mirror one day.

At a seminar I was presenting at, a group of executives were standing around enjoying a cup of coffee in the break. One of them had just come back from a visit to the Golden Door health retreat in the Hunter Valley, just outside Sydney. When asked by the group what it was like, he said that it was great and that he felt recharged, he knew he looked better, he had the twinkle back in his eye and health-wise he felt 100 per cent better.

Make sure you take the time to do just this—breathe, relax and think...

He went on to recall the moment he had agreed to go to the resort. He had gone to visit his daughter for dinner, and as he walked in the front door, she said, 'Dad, what's wrong with you? You look like shit'. He said at that point he took a good look at himself and realised that he was working too hard, was too stressed, was unhealthy and was digging himself into an early grave. It was then that he decided to make some adjustments. You have to love the honesty of our children!

On another occasion when I was a guest speaker I heard the CEO of a large global firm talking about the success his business was having. He mentioned the countries he was visiting, how much time he was spending on a plane, the acquisitions his company was making and how the company was achieving its targets—but not without a lot of hard work. He talked about the future, more acquisitions, more stress, more hard work and more time sitting in a business class seat of a Qantas plane. One of his mates asked how his family was and he said, 'Well, my young son has gone through some anxiety attacks and stopped eating for a couple of weeks, but I think we're through that now and he's okay'. The guys with him chuckled and joked that his son was probably anxious because he didn't know who his dad was. The executive replied, 'Oh no, I talk to him via Skype and on the telephone, so I've got that covered'. This is one guy who definitely needs to take a good look in the mirror.

Recently, I was giving a speech and I asked the audience to reflect on the year gone by and some of the lessons they had taken from that time. One audience member, who was a mum, stood up and said, 'I've learned this year that I need to breathe'. She said so often she is buzzing around the house, trying to take care of family, business, phone calls and computers, and then one day, her three-year-old daughter stopped her and said, 'Breathe, Mummy, breathe'. She said, 'I realised I was spinning out of control and my daughter was absolutely correct. I wasn't taking time to breathe, relax and think'. Make sure you take the time to do just this—breathe, relax and think—before you find you don't have much of a relationship with your kids.

Dad's fallen off the wagon

There's been a lot written in these pages for you to consider and/or put into action. However, there are some times when it's just not possible. There are times when even the most outstanding of dads needs to dig in for a pitch, a tender document or when a crisis strikes at work. We all know that sometimes poo happens and we need to sort it out. As long as it's the minority of your time and not the majority, then that's cool. Children need to learn that this is going to happen. If dad's fallen off the wagon, then it should be just that. It's when dads can't see the light at the end of the tunnel once they've fallen off the wagon, or they spend their entire time off the wagon, that it becomes an issue.

We're only human, and sometimes we need to get things done for whatever reason. Just make sure it's the exception more than the rule. If some sort of crisis does happen, it's important that you explain it to your children and your wife or partner. Let them know what the expected actions are going to have to be, how long it's going to go on for and what's likely to happen when you get through this period. Kids get it. Wives and partners … should get it. Just remember, dads, you don't need to be perfect, and if you're holding yourself to a standard of being truly outstanding, when these things happen you'll be able to work your way through them and it will be all good.

They're not yours

Before Charley was born I read a book called *Secrets of the Baby Whisperer* by Tracy Hogg, and one comment the author made had a big impact on me. Hogg discusses the fact that although you are going to have a child, ultimately, he's not yours. At first I thought this was a bit odd, but when I read further, I realised she meant that although you are having a baby, he's not yours in that you don't own him and your responsibility is not to have him grow up and be like you.

Your responsibility is to create a caring, warm, loving environment for your child...

Your responsibility is to create a caring, warm, loving environment for your child for him to grow up to be the best he can be in whatever he chooses to do.

I always hear of parents putting pressure on children to grow up to be the same as them, or the same as them only not making the same mistakes. Children are born geniuses. It's all the stuff we do to them that takes the genius away. Our job is to create the right environment to teach them right from wrong, safe from unsafe, and what's acceptable and unacceptable. Apart from that just step back and help them in whichever way you can for them to grow up to be the best they can be in whatever field or endeavour they choose to pursue. As they grow, they will know what their own purpose in life is. Our job is not to colour them, push them or design it for them; our job is to make it safe, curious, stimulating and encouraging. They will make up their own mind.

When I read *Secrets of the Baby Whisperer* it made a lot of sense to me and it changed my approach to being a dad.

We have to cherish children for who they are instead of for what we want them to be.

A few things to consider

I'm going to finish with a couple more things for you to consider. First, this trend of play and curiosity, and giving children time and room to explore and make mistakes is not just a trend among parents, but also governments. Many governments around the world have started to make more room for creativity, play and rest in school systems. Many schools are beginning to understand that it's more important for children to think outside the box than to tick the box. It's a pity more businesses aren't learning from schools and children.

Second, Marilee Jones, a former dean of admissions at the Massachusetts Institute of Technology, made an interesting comment in Carl Honoré's book *Under Pressure*. She explained that children thrive when they have the time and space to breathe, to hang out and get bored sometimes, to relax, to take risks and make mistakes, to dream and have fun on their own terms, even to fail. She went on to say that if we are going to restore the joy not only to childhood but to parenthood too, then the time has come for adults to back off a little and allow children to be themselves. This is the beginning of a revolution.

...it's more important for children to think outside the box than to tick the box.

When parents do back off and give children the chance to create and even make mistakes, then children are giving themselves texture and ultimately giving a meaning to their own life. Their small adventures, secret dreams, play and mimicry during times of solitude and even boredom give fuel to their imagination, which is one of the greatest gifts that we as parents can give to our children. It is the gift of thinking differently.

Here's a reminder of some things we can do as parents to help our children be the best they can be:

- *Back off*. Don't try to take over everything. Allow children to draw a face the way that they want to draw a face. Don't always correct their creativity and imagination.

- *Give them time*. Allow children time by themselves to play. Don't think that play is a mindless waste of time.

- *Engage in true conversation with them*. Don't talk down to your children, get down to the same level as them and look them in the eye. If you've never seen what it's like to be a two or three year old, then go to the supermarket, crouch down and walk through the aisles on your knees and see how scary it is to look up. Your level of communication, understanding and engagement is enhanced when you lower yourself in physical stature to truly look into the eyes of your children.

- ◻ *Be curious*. Ask children as many open-ended questions as they ask you. There's enormous power in questioning and having children think. When they imagine a story or you read them a story, ask them questions about it and get their perspective. Ask questions within questions to truly have them dig down and get in touch with their thinking.

- ◻ *Listen to their opinions*. Disconnect from technology and the outside world and engage with your children. Listen to their opinions as if their opinion was the most important thing in the world. Give them the respect that you give the people that you work with or for. Engage and ask them questions about their opinions. Don't edit them, don't correct them, don't try to offer an opinion about their opinion, just listen and fuel curiosity with more questions.

This book is not designed to make you the perfect parent, but it is my hope that it will put you on the road to being an outstanding dad! As Vince Lombardi said, 'Perfection is not attainable, but if we chase perfection, we can catch excellence'. So when you come home at night, check yourself at the front door, disconnect, really engage and enjoy the gift you've been privileged to be a part of, which is watching your children grow.

If you're not yet convinced that there's value in building a great relationship with your children, then perhaps this final comment will provide the necessary evidence.

The authors of *A Good Childhood*, Richard Layard and Judy Dunn, believe that if children are in conflict with their fathers or find them harsh or neglectful they are much more likely to become destructive and aggressive themselves. As dads we carry a lot of responsibility!

Further reading

Daniel G Amen, *Magnificent Mind at Any Age: Natural Ways to Unleash Your Brain's Maximum Potential*, Crown Publishing Group, 2009.

William C Crain, *Reclaiming Childhood: Letting Children Be Children in Our Achievement-Oriented Society*, Henry Holt and Company, 2003.

Lise Eliot, *What's Going on in There? How the Brain and Mind Develop in the First Five Years of Life*, Random House Publishing Group, 2000.

Jeff Grout and Sarah Perrin, *Mind Games: Inspirational Lessons from the World's Finest Sports Stars*, John Wiley & Sons, 2006.

Kathy Hirsh-Pasek and Roberta Michnick Golinkoff, *Einstein Never Used Flash Cards: How Our Children Really Learn—and Why They Need to Play More and Memorize Less*, Rodale Books, 2004.

Tracy Hogg, *Secrets of the Baby Whisperer: How to Calm, Connect, and Communicate with Your Baby*, Random House Publishing Group, 2005.

Carl Honoré, *Under Pressure: Rescuing Our Children from the Culture of Hyper-Parenting*, HarperCollins Publishers, 2009.

Richard Layard and Judy Dunn, *A Good Childhood: Searching for Values in a Competitive Age*, Penguin Books, 2009.

Judith Rich Harris, *The Nurture Assumption: Why Children Turn Out the Way They Do*, Free Press, 2009.

Ken Robinson, *The Element: How Finding Your Passion Changes Everything*, Penguin, 2009.

Martin Seligman, *The Optimistic Child: A Revolutionary Approach to Raising Resilient Children*, Random House Australia, 1995.

Index

Notes

Notes

Notes

Notes

Gary
BERTWIST E

Unlock your great ideas

Visit <www.garybertwistle.com> for information about Gary's keynote speeches to unlock your great ideas. There are free podcasts, vidcasts, the latest news and a free subscription to *The Espresso*, the world's first newspaper for thinkers. Have *The Espresso* delivered free to your desktop every Wednesday! You'll also find information about Gary's venue, The Idea's Vault, a place to think differently in Sydney.